The

GLORY
of
CHRIST

Table of Contents

CHAPTER 1
The Fullness of Christ

It is fitting that we should contemplate the excellencies of Christ the Mediator, for "the light of the knowledge of the glory of God" is to be seen "in the face of Jesus Christ" (2 Cor. 4:6). The fullest revelation that God is and what He is, is made in the person of Christ. "No man hath seen God at any time; the only begotten Son, which is in the bosom of the Father, he hath declared" (1 John 1:18). But this knowledge of God is not a mere matter of intellectual apprehension, which one man can communicate to another. But it is a spiritual discernment, imparted by the Holy Spirit. God must shine in our hearts to give us that knowledge.

When the materialistic Philip said, "Lord, show us the Father," the Lord Jesus replied, "he that hath seen me hath seen the Father" (John 14:9). Yes, He was "the brightness of His glory, and the express image of His person" (Heb. 1:3). In the eternal, incarnate Word "dwelleth all the fullness of the Godhead bodily" (Col. 2:9). Amazing and glorious fact, it is in the perfection of manhood that the fullness of the Godhead is in Christ revealed to our faith. We could not ascend to God, so He descended to us. All that men can ever know of God is presented to them in the person of His incarnate Son. Hence, "That I may know him" (Phil. 3:10) is the constant longing of the most mature Christian.

It is our design to declare some part of that glory of our Lord Jesus Christ which is revealed in Scripture, and proposed as the object of our faith, love, delight, admiration and adoration. But after our utmost endeavors and most diligent inquiries we have to say, "How little a portion" (Job 26:14) of Him we understand. His glory is incomprehensible, His praises unutterable. Some things a divinely illuminated mind can conceive of, but what we express, in comparison to what the glory is in itself, is less than nothing. Nevertheless, that view which the Spirit grants from the Scriptures concerning Christ and His glory is to be preferred above all other knowledge or understanding. So it was declared, by him who was favored to know Him, "Yea doubtless, and I count all things but loss for the excellency of the knowledge of Christ Jesus my Lord" (Phil. 3:8).

John Owen has well said:

The revelation made of Christ in the blessed Gospel is far more excellent, more glorious, more filled with rays of Divine wisdom and goodness than the whole creation, and the just comprehension of it, if attainable, can contain or apprehend. Without the knowledge hereof, the mind of man, however priding itself in other inventions and discoveries, is wrapped up in darkness and confusion. This therefore deserves the severest of our thoughts, the best of our meditations, and our utmost diligence in them. For if our future blessedness shall consist in living where He is, and beholding of His glory; what better preparation can there be for it, than in a constant previous contemplation of that glory, in the revelation that is made in the Gospel unto this very end, that by a view of it we may be gradually transformed into the same glory.

The grandest of all privileges which believers are capable of, either in this world or the next, is to behold the glory (the personal and official excellencies) of Christ; now by faith, then by sight. Equally certain, no man will ever behold the glory of Christ by sight in heaven, who does not now behold it by faith. Where the soul has not been previously purified by grace and faith, it is incapable of glory and the open vision. Those who pretend to be greatly enamored by or to ardently desire that which they never saw or experienced, only dote on their imaginations. The pretended desires of many (especially on deathbeds) to behold the glory of Christ in heaven, but who had no vision of it by faith while they were in this world, are nothing but self-deceiving delusions.

There is no true rest for the mind nor satisfaction for the heart until we rest in Christ (Matthew 11:28-30). God has proposed to us the "mystery of godliness," that is, the person of His incarnate Son and His mediatorial work, as the supreme object of our faith and meditation. In this "mystery" we are called upon to behold the highest exhibition of the divine wisdom, goodness, and condescension. The Son of God assumed manhood by union with Himself, thereby constituting the same person in two natures, yet infinitely distinct as those of God and man. Thereby the Infinite became finite, the Eternal temporal, and the Immortal mortal, yet continued still infinite, eternal and immortal.

It cannot be expected that those who are drowned in the love of the world will have any true apprehension of Christ, or any real desire for it. But for those who have "tasted that the Lord is gracious" (1 Pet. 2:3), how foolish we would be if we gave all our time and strength to other things, to the neglect of diligent searching of Scripture to obtain a fuller knowledge of Him.

Man is "born to trouble as the sparks fly upward," but the same Scriptures reveal a divinely appointed relief from all the evils to which fallen man is heir—so that we may not faint under them, but gain the victory over them.

Listen to the testimony of one who passed through a far deeper sea of trial than the great majority of men: We are troubled on every side, yet not distressed; we are perplexed, but not in despair; persecuted, but not forsaken; cast down, but not destroyed . . . For which cause we faint not: but though our outward man perish, yet the inward is renewed day by day. For our light affliction, which is but for a moment, worketh for us a far more exceeding and eternal weight of glory: while we look not at the things which are seen . . . but the things which are not seen are eternal (2 Cor. 4:8; 4:16-18).

It is beholding by faith things which "are not seen" by the eye (which the spiritually poverty-stricken occupants of palaces and millionaire mansions know nothing of), the things that are spiritual and eternal, which alleviates the Christian's afflictions. Of these unseen, eternal things the supernal glories of Christ are the principal. He who can contemplate Him who is "the Lord of glory," will, when "all around gives way," be lifted out of himself and delivered from the prevailing power of evil.

Not until the mind arrives at a fixed judgment that all things here are transitory and reach only to outward man—that everything under the sun is but "vanity and vexation of spirit," and there are other things incalculably better to comfort and satisfy the heart—not till then will we ever be delivered from spending our lives in fear, distress, and sorrow. Christ alone can satisfy the heart. And when He does truly satisfy, the language of the soul is, "Whom have I in heaven but thee? and there is none upon earth that I desire beside thee" (Ps. 73:25).

How slight and shadowy, how petty and puerile are those things from which the trials of men arise! They all grow from the one root of the over-valuation of temporal things. Money cannot purchase joy of soul. Health does not insure happiness. A beautiful home will not satisfy the heart. Earthly friends, no matter how loyal and loving, cannot speak peace to a sin-burdened conscience, nor impart eternal life. Envy, covetousness, discontent, receive their death wound when Christ, in all His loveliness, is revealed as the "chiefest among ten thousand" (Song 5:10).

CHAPTER 2
The Radiance of Christ

The law had "a shadow of good things to come" (Heb. 10:1). A beautiful illustration of this is in the closing verses of Exodus 34, where Moses descends from the mount with a radiant face. The key to the passage is found in noting the exact position it occupies in this book of redemption. It comes after the legal covenant which Jehovah made with Israel; it comes before the actual setting up of the tabernacle and the Shekinah glory filling it. This passage is interpreted in 2 Corinthians 3. Exodus 34 supplies both a comparison and a contrast with the new dispensation of the Spirit, of grace, of life more abundant. But before that dispensation was inaugurated God saw fit for man to be tested under Law, to demonstrate what he is as a fallen and sinful creature.

Man's trial under the Mosaic economy demonstrated two things: first, that he is "ungodly"; second, that he is "without strength" (Rom. 5:6). But these are negative things. Romans 8:7 mentions a third feature of man's terrible state, namely, that he is "enmity against God." This was manifest when God's Son tabernacled for thirty-three years on this earth. "He came unto his own, and his own received Him not" (John 1:11). Not only so, but also He was "despised and rejected of men." Nay, more, they hated Him "without a cause" (John 15:25). Nor could their hatred be appeased until they had condemned Him to a malefactor's death and nailed Him to the cross. Remember it was not only the Jews who put to death the Lord of glory, but also the Gentiles. Therefore the Lord said, when looking forward to His death, "Now is the judgment of this world" (John 12:31), not of Israel only. There the probation or testing of man ended.

Man is not now under probation; he is under condemnation: "As it is written, There is none righteous, no, not one: there is none that understandeth, there is none that seeketh after God. They are all gone out of the way, they are together become unprofitable; there is none that doeth good, no, not one" (Rom. 3:10-12). Man is not on trial; he is a culprit under sentence. No pleading will avail; no excuses will be accepted. The present issue between God and the sinner is, will man bow to God's righteous verdict?

This is where the Gospel meets us. It comes to us as to those who are already lost, to those who are "ungodly," "without strength," "enmity against God." It announces to us the amazing grace of God, the only hope for poor sinners. But grace will not be welcomed until the sinner bows to the sentence of God against him. That is why both repentance and faith are demanded from the sinner. These two must not be separated. Paul preached "repentance toward God. and faith toward our Lord Jesus Christ" (Acts 20:21). Repentance is the sinner's acknowledgement of that sentence of condemnation under which he lives. Faith is acceptance of the grace and mercy extended to him through Christ. Repentance is not turning over a new leaf and vowing to mend our ways. Rather it is setting to my seal that God is true when He tells me I am "without strength," that in myself my case is hopeless, that I am no more able to "do better next time" than I am to create a world. Not until this is really believed (not as the result of experience, but on the authority of God's Word) shall we really turn to Christ and welcome Him —not as a Helper, but as a Savior.

As it was dispensationally, so it is experimentally. There must be "a ministration of death" (2 Cor. 3:7) before there is a "ministration of spirit" or life (2 Cor. 3:8): there must be "the ministration of condemnation" before "the ministration of righteousness" (2 Cor. 3:9). A "ministration of condemnation and death" falls strangely on our ears, does it not? A "ministration of grace" we can understand: but a "ministration of condemnation" is not so easy to grasp. But this latter was man's first need. He must be shown what he is in himself—a hopeless wreck, utterly incapable of meeting the righteous requirements of a holy God—before he is ready to be a debtor to mercy alone. We repeat: as it was dispensationally, so it is experimentally. It was to his own experience that the apostle Paul referred when he said, "For I was alive without the law once: but when the commandment came, sin revived, and I died" (Rom. 7:9). In his unregenerate days he was, in his own estimation, "alive," yet it was "without the law," apart from meeting its demands. "But when the commandment came," when the Holy Spirit wrought within him, when the Word of God came in power to his heart, then "sin revived." He was made aware of his awful condition, and then he "died" to his self-righteous complacency. He saw that, in himself, his case was hopeless. Yes, the appearing of the glorified Mediator comes not before, but after, the legal covenant.

"And he was there with the Lord forty days and forty nights; he did neither eat bread, nor drink water. And he wrote upon the tables the words of the covenant, the ten commandments" (Ex. 34:28). Our passage abounds in comparisons and contrasts. The "forty days" here at once recalls the "forty days" in Matthew 4. Here it was Moses; there it was Christ. Here it was Moses on the mount; there it was Christ in the wilderness. Here it was Moses favored with a glorious revelation from God; there it was Christ being tempted of the devil. Here it was Moses receiving the Law at the mouth of Jehovah; there it was Christ being assailed by the devil to repudiate that Law. We scarcely know which is the greater wonder of the two: that a sinful man was raised to such a height of honor as to spend a season in the presence of the great Jehovah, or that the Lord of glory. Should stoop so low as to be for six weeks with the foul friend.

"And it came to pass, when Moses came down from mount Sinai with the two tables of testimony in Moses' hand, when he came down from the mount, that Moses wist not that the skin of his face shown while he talked with him" (Ex. 34:29). Blessed it is to compare and contrast this second descent of Moses from the mount with what is before us in chapter 32. There the face of Moses is diffused with anger (v. 19); here he comes down with countenance radiant. There he beheld a people engaged in idolatry; here he returns to a people abashed. There we behold him dashing the tables of stone to the ground (v. 19); here he deposits them in the ark (Deut. 10:5).

This event also reminds us of a New Testament episode, very similar, yet dissimilar. It was on the mount that the face of Moses was made radiant, and it was on the mount that our Lord was transfigured. But the glory of Moses was only a reflected one, whereas that of Christ was inherent. The shining of Moses' face was the consequence of his being brought into the immediate presence of the glory of Jehovah; the transfiguration of Christ was the outshining of His own personal glory. The radiance of Moses was confined to his face, but of Christ we read, "His raiment was white as the light" (Matthew 17:2). Moses "knew not" that the skin of his face shone; Christ did, evident from His words, "Tell the vision to no man" (Matthew 17:9).

Verse 29 brings out what is the certain consequence of intimate communion with the Lord, and in a twofold way. First, no soul can enjoy real fellowship with God without being affected by it to a marked degree.

Moses had been absorbed in the communications received and in contemplating His glory. His own person caught and retained some of the beams of that glory. So it is still (Ps. 34:5, R.V.), "They looked upon Him, and their faces were radiant." It is communion with the Lord that conforms us to His image. We shall not be more Christlike until we walk more frequently and more closely with Him. "But we all, with open face beholding as in a glass the glory of the Lord, are changed into the same image from glory to glory, even as by the Spirit of the Lord" (2 Cor. 3:18).

The second consequence of real communion with God is that we will be less occupied with ourselves. Though Moses' face shone with "a light not seen on land or sea," he did not know it. This illustrates a vital difference between self-righteous Pharisaism and true godliness; the former produces complacency and pride, the latter leads to self-abnegation and humility. The Pharisee (there are many of his tribe still on earth) boasts of his attainments, advertises his imaginary spirituality, and thanks God he is not as other men. But the one who, by grace, enjoys much fellowship with the Lord learns of Him who was "meek and lowly in heart," and says, "Not unto us, O LORD, not unto us, but unto thy name give glory" (Ps. 115:1). Engaged with the beauty of the Lord, he is delivered from self-occupation, and is therefore unconscious of the very fruit of the Spirit being brought forth in him. But though he is not aware of his increasing conformity to Christ, others are.

"And when Aaron and all the children of Israel saw Moses, behold, the skin of his face shone; and they were afraid to come nigh him" (Ex. 34:30). This shows us the third effect of communion with God. Though the individual himself is unconscious of the glory manifested through him, others recognize it. Thus it was when two of Christ's apostles stood before the Jewish Sanhedrin: "Now when they saw the boldness of Peter and John, and perceived that they were unlearned and ignorant men, they marveled; and they took knowledge of them, that they had been with Jesus" (Acts 4:13, italics added). We cannot keep company very long with the Holy One without His imprint being left upon us. The man who is thoroughly devoted to the Lord does not need to wear some badge in his coat lapel, nor to proclaim that he is "living a life of victory." It is still true that actions speak louder than words.

"And when Aaron and all the children of Israel saw Moses, behold, the skin of His face shone; and they were afraid to come nigh him." The typical meaning of this is given in 2 Corinthians 3:7, "But if the ministration of death, written and engraven in stones, was glorious, so that the children of Israel could not stedfastly behold the face of Moses for the glory of his countenance." Concerning this, Ed Dennett has said: Why, then, were they afraid to come near him? Because the very glory that shone upon his face searched their hearts and consciences—being what they were, sinners, and unable of themselves to meet even the smallest requirements of the covenant which had now been inaugurated. It was of necessity a 'ministration' of condemnation and death, for it required a righteousness from them which they could not render, and inasmuch as they must fail in the rendering it, would pronounce their condemnation, and bring them under the penalty of transgression, which was death. The glory which they thus beheld upon the face of Moses was the expression to them of the holiness of God—that holiness which sought from them conformity to its own standards, and which would vindicate the breaches of that covenant which had now been established. They were therefore afraid because they knew in their inmost souls that they could not stand before Him from whose presence Moses had come.

Typically the covenant Jehovah made with Moses and Israel at Sinai, and the tables of stone on which the ten commandments were engraved, foreshadowed a new covenant.

For I will take you from among the heathen, and gather you out of all countries, and will bring you into your own land. Then will I sprinkle clean water upon you, and ye shall be clean: from all your filthiness, and from all your idols, will I cleanse you. A new heart also will I give you, and a new spirit will I put within you: and I will take away the stony heart out of your flesh, and I will give you an heart of flesh. And I will put my spirit within you, and cause you to walk in my statutes, and ye shall keep my judgments, and do them. And ye shall dwell in the land that I gave to your fathers; and ye shall be my people, and I will be your God (Ezek. 36:24-28).

Behold, the days come, saith the LORD, that I will make a new covenant with the house of Israel, and with the house of Judah . . . After those days, saith the LORD, I will put my law in their inward parts, and write in their hearts . . . And they shall teach no more every man his neighbor, and every man his brother, saying, Know the LORD: for they shall all know me, from the least of them unto the greatest of them, saith the Lord (Jer. 31:31-34).

Spiritually, this is made good for Christians even now. Under the gracious operations of the Spirit of God our hearts have been made plastic and receptive. Paul refers to this at the beginning of 2 Corinthians 3.

The saints at Corinth had been manifested to be Christ's epistle ministered by us, written not with ink, but with the Spirit of the living God, not on stone tables, but on fleshy tables of the heart. Their hearts being made impressionable by Divine working, Christ could write upon them, using Paul as a pen, and making every mark in the power of the Spirit of God. But what is written is the knowledge of God as revealed through the Mediator in the grace of the new covenant, so that it might be true in the hearts of the saints —"They shall all know Me." Then Paul goes on to speak of himself as made competent by God to be a new covenant ministry, "not of the letter, but of the spirit." (C. A. Coates).

"And Moses called unto them; and Aaron and all the rulers of the congregation returned unto him; and Moses talked with them. And afterward all the children of Israel came nigh: and he gave them in commandment all that the LORD had spoken with him in Mount Sinai. And till Moses had done speaking with them, he put a vail on his face" (Ex. 34:31-33). Does not this explain their fear as they beheld the shine of Moses' face? Note what was in his hands! He carried the two tables of stone on which were written the ten words of the Law, the "ministration of condemnation." The nearer the light of the glory came, while it was connected with the righteous claims of God upon them, the more cause they had to fear. That holy Law condemned them, for man in the flesh could not meet its claims. "However blessed it was typically, it was literally a ministry of death, for Moses was not a quickening spirit, nor could he give his spirit to the people, nor could the glory of his face bring them into conformity with himself as the mediator. Hence the veil had to be on his face" (C. A. Coates).

The dispensational interpretation of this is given in 2 Corinthians 3:13: "And not as Moses, which put a vail over his face, that the children of Israel could not stedfastly look to the end of that which is abolished." Here the apostle treats of Judaism as an economy. Owing to their spiritual blindness Israel was unable to discern the deep significance of the ministry of Moses, or the purpose of God behind it, that to which all the types and shadows pointed. The "end" of 2 Corinthians 3:13, is parallel with Romans 10:4, "For Christ is the end of the law for righteousness to every one that believeth."

The veil on Israel's heart is self-sufficiency, which makes them still refuse to submit to God's righteousness. But when Israel's heart turns to the Lord the veil will be taken away. What a wonderful chapter Exodus 34 will be to them then! For they will see that Christ is the spirit of it all. What they will see, we are privileged to see now. All this had an "end" on which we can, through infinite grace, fix our eyes. The "end" was the glory of the Lord as the Mediator of the new covenant. He has come out of death and gone up on high, and the glory of all that God is in grace is shining in His face (C. A. Coates).

"But when Moses went in before the LORD to speak with him, he took the vail off, until he came out. And he came out, and spake unto the children of Israel that which he was commanded. And the children of Israel saw the face of Moses, that the skin of Moses' face shone: and Moses put the vail upon his face again, until he went in to speak with him" (v. 34-35). Moses unveiled in the presence of the Lord is a beautiful type of the believer of this dispensation. The Christian beholds the glory of God shining in the face of Jesus Christ (2 Cor. 4:6). Therefore, instead of being stricken with fear, he approaches with boldness. God's Law cannot condemn him, for its every demand has been fully met and satisfied by his Substitute. Hence, instead of trembling before the glory of God, we "rejoice in hope of the glory of God" (Rom. 5:2).

There is no veil now either on His face or our hearts. He makes those who believe on Him to live in the knowledge of God, and in response to God, for He is the quickening Spirit. And He gives His Spirit to those who believe. We have the Spirit of the glorious Man in whose face the glory of God shines. Is it not wonderful? One has to ask, Do we really believe it? But we all, looking on the glory of the Lord with unveiled face, are transformed according to the same image from glory to glory, even as by the Lord the Spirit (2 Cor. 3:18). If we had not His Spirit we should have no liberty to look on the glory of the Lord, or to see Him as the Spirit of these marvelous types. But we have liberty to look on it all, and there is transforming power in it. Saints under the new covenant ministry are transfigured.

This is the 'surpassing glory' which could not be seen or known until it shone in the face of Him of whom Moses in Exodus 34 is so distinctly a type. The whole typical system was temporary, but its 'spirit' abides, for Christ was the Spirit of it all. Now we have to do with the ministry of the new covenant subsists and abounds in glory (C. A. Coates).

The authority of Paul's apostleship had been called into question by certain Judaizers. In the first verses of 2 Corinthians 3 he appeals to the Christians there as the proof of his God-commissioned ministry. He defines the character of his ministry (v. 6) to show its superiority over that of his enemies. He and his fellow gospelers were "ministers of the new testament" or covenant. He then draws a series of contrasts between the two covenants, Judaism and Christianity. What pertained to the old is called "the letter," and that relating to the new "the spirit." One was mainly concerned with what was external, the other was largely internal; the one slew, the other gave life, one of the leading differences between the Law and the Gospel.

In what follows, the apostle, while allowing the Law was glorious, shows that the Gospel is still more glorious. The old covenant was a "ministration of death," for the Law could only condemn. Therefore, though a glory was connected with it, yet it was such that man in the flesh could not behold (v. 7). Then how much more excellent would be, must be, the glory of the new covenant, seeing it was "a ministration of the spirit" (v. 8). Compare verse 3 for proof of this. If there were a glory connected with what "concluded all under sin" (Gal. 3:22), much more glorious that ministration must be which announced a righteousness "unto all and upon all them that believe" (Rom. 3:22). It is more glorious to pardon than to condemn; to give life than to destroy (v. 9). The glory of the former covenant therefore pales into nothingness before the latter (v. 10), further seen from the fact Judaism is "done away," whereas Christianity "remaineth" (v. 11). Compare Hebrews 8:7-8.

The apostle draws still another contrast (v. 12) between the two economies, namely the plainness or perspicuity over against the obscurity and ambiguity of their respective ministries (vv. 12-15). The apostle used "great plainness of speech," while the teaching of the ceremonial law was by shadows and symbols. Moreover, the minds of the Israelites were blinded, so that there was a veil over their eyes. Therefore, when the writings of Moses were read they were incapable of looking beyond the type to the Antitype. This veil remains upon them to this day, and will continue until they turn to the Lord (vv. 15-16). Literally the covenant of Sinai was a ministration of condemnation and death, and the glory of it had to be veiled. But it had an "end" (v. 13) which Israel could not see. They will see that end in a coming day. But in the meantime we are permitted to read the old covenant without a veil, and to see that Christ is the "spirit" of it all.

The language of verse 17 is somewhat obscure: "Now the Lord is that Spirit," which does not mean that Christ is the Holy Spirit. The "spirit" here is the same as in verse 6, "not of the letter, but of the spirit" (cf. Romans

7:6). The Mosaic system is called "the letter" because it was purely objective and possessed no inward principle or power. But the Gospel deals with the heart, and supplies the spiritual power (Rom. 1:16). Moreover, Christ is the spirit, the life, the heart and center of all the ritual and ceremonialism of Judaism. He is the key to the Old Testament, for "in the volume of the book" it is written of Him. So also Christ is the spirit and life of Christianity. He is "a quickening spirit" (1 Cor. 15:45). And "where the Spirit of the Lord is, there is liberty." Apart from Christ, the sinner, be he Jew or Gentile, is in bondage; he is the slave of sin and the captive of the devil. But where the Son makes free, He frees indeed (John 8:32).

Finally, the apostle contrasts the two glories, the glory connected with the old covenant—the shining on Moses' face at the giving of the Law with the glory of the new covenant, in the person of Christ. "But we all, with open [unveiled] face beholding as in a glass the glory of the Lord, are changed into the same image from glory to glory, even as by the Spirit of the Lord." Note here, first, "we all." Moses alone beheld the glory of the Lord in the mount; every Christian now beholds it. Second, "with open face," with freedom and with confidence; whereas Israel was afraid to gaze on the radiant and majestical face of Moses. Third, we are "changed into the same image." The law had no power to convert or purify; but the ministry of the Gospel, under the operation of the Spirit, has a transforming power. Those who are saved by it and who are occupied with Christ as set forth in the Word (the "mirror"), are, little by little, conformed to His image. Ultimately, when we "see him as he is" (1 John 3:2), we shall be "like him"—full, perfectly, eternally.

CHAPTER 3
The Condescension of Christ

For the sake of accuracy, a distinction should be drawn between the condescension and the humiliation of Christ, though most writers confound them. This distinction is made by the Holy Spirit (Phil. 2:7-8). First, He "made himself of no reputation": second, He "humbled himself." The condescension of God the Son consisted in His assuming our nature, the Word becoming flesh. His humiliation lay in the consequent abasement and sufferings He endured in our nature. The assumption of human nature was not, of itself, a part of Christ's humiliation, for He still retained it in His glorious exaltation. But for God the Son to take into union with Himself a created nature, animated dust, was an act of infinite condescension.

Who, being in the form of God, thought it not robbery to be equal with God: but made himself of no reputation, and took upon him the form of a servant, and was made in the likeness of men: and being found in fashion as a man, he humbled himself, and became obedient unto death, even the death of the cross. Wherefore God also hath highly exalted him, and given him a name which is above every name (Phil. 2:6-9).

These verses trace the path of the Mediator from highest glory to deepest humiliation, and back again to His supreme honor. What a wondrous path was His! And how terrible that this divine description of His path should have become the battleground of theological contention. At few points has the awful depravity of man's heart been more horribly displayed than by the blasphemies vented upon these verses.

A glance at the context (Phil. 2:1-5) at once shows the practical design of the apostle was to exhort Christians to spiritual fellowship among themselves —to be likeminded, to love one another, to be humble and lowly, to esteem others better than themselves. To enforce this, the example of our Lord is proposed in the verses we now consider. We are to have the same mind in us that was in Him; the mind, spirit, habit, of self-abnegation, the mind of self-sacrifice, and of obedience to God. We must humble ourselves beneath the mighty hand of God, if we are to be exalted by Him in due time (1 Pet. 5:6). To set before us the example of Christ in its most vivid colors, the Holy Spirit takes us back to the position which our Mediator occupied in eternity. He shows us that supreme dignity and glory was His, then reminds us of those unfathomable depths of condescension and humiliation into which He descended for our sakes.

"Who being in the form of God." First of all, this affirms the absolute Deity of the Son, for no mere creature, no matter how high in the scale of being, could ever be "in the form of God." Three words are used concerning the Sons' relation to the Godhead. First, He subsists in the "form" of God, seen in Him alone. Second, He is "the image of the invisible God" (Col. 1:15), which expression tells of His manifestation of God to us (cf. 2 Corinthians 4:6). Third, He is the "brightness of his glory and the express image of his person" (Heb. 1:3), or more exactly, the "effulgency (outshining) of His glory and the exact Expression of His substance" (Bagster Interlinear). These perhaps combine both concepts suggested by form and image, namely, that the whole nature of God is in Christ, that by Him God is declared and expressed to us.

"Who being," or subsisting (it is hardly correct to speak of a divine person "existing." He is self-existent; He always was in "the form of God." "Form" (the Greek word is only found elsewhere in the New Testament in Philippians 2:7, Mark 16:12) is what is apparent. "The form of God" is an expression which seems to denote His visible glory, His displayed majesty, His manifested sovereignty. From eternity the Son was clothed with all the insignia of deity, adorned with all divine splendor. "The Word was God" (John 1:1).

"Thought it not robbery to be equal with God." Almost every word in this verse has been the occasion of contention. But we have sufficient confidence in the superintending providence of God to be satisfied the translators of our authorized version were preserved from any serious mistake on a subject so vitally important. As the first clause of our verse refers to an objective delineation of the divine dignity of the Son, so this second clause affirms His subjective consciousness. The word "thought" is used (here in the aorist tense) to indicate a definite point in time past. The word rendered "robbery" denotes not the spoil or prize, but the act of taking the spoil. The Son did not reckon equality with the Father and the Holy Spirit an act of usurping.

"Thought it not robbery to be equal with God." This is only a negative way to say that Christ considered equality with God as what justly and essentially belonged to Him. It was His by indisputable right. Christ esteemed such equality as no invasion of Another's prerogative, but regarded Himself as being entitled to all divine honors. Because He held the rank of one of the Three coeternal, coessential, and co-glorious persons of the Godhead, the Son reckoned His full and perfect equality with the other two was His unchallengeable portion. In Verse 6 is no doubt a latent reference to Satan's fall. He, though "the anointed cherub" (Ezek. 28:14), was infinitely below God, yet he grasped at equality with Him. "I will ascend above the heights of the clouds, I will be like the most High" (Isa. 14:14).

However the Greek word for "robbery" is translated, it is evident the emphatic term of this clause is "equal." For if it signifies a real and proper equality, then the proof for the absolute deity of the Savior is irrefutable. How, then, is the exact significance of this term to be determined? Not by having recourse to Homer, nor any other heathen writer, but by discovering the meaning of its cognate. If we can fix the precise rendering of the adjective, then we may be sure of the adverb. The adjective is found in several passages (Matthew 20:12; Luke 6:34; John 5:18; Acts 11:17; Revelation 21:6). In each passage the reference is not to a likeness only, but to a real and proper equality! Thus the force of this clause is parallel with, "I and my Father are one" (John 10:30).

"My Father is greater than I" (John 14:28) must not be allowed to negate John 10:30. There are no contradictions in Holy Writ. Each of these passages may be given its full force without there being any conflict between them. The simple way to discover their perfect consistency is to remember, that Scripture exhibits our Savior in two chief characters: as God the Son, the second Person of the Trinity; and as Mediator, the God-man, the Word become flesh. In the former, He is described as possessing all the perfections of deity; in the latter, as the Servant of the Godhead. Speaking of Himself according to His essential Being, He could unqualifiedly say, "I and Father are one,"—one in essence or nature. Speaking of Himself according to His mediatorial office, He could say, "My Father is greater than I," not essentially, but economically.

Each expression used (Phil. 2:6) is expressly designed by the Holy Spirit to magnify the divine dignity of Christ's person. He is the Possesser of a glory equal with God's, with an unquestioned right to that glory, deeming it no robbery to challenge it. His glory is not an accidental or phenomenal one, but a substantial and essential one, subsisting in the very "form of God." Between what is Infinite and what is finite, what is Eternal and what is temporal, He who is the Creator and what is the creature, it is utterly impossible there should be any equality. "To whom then will ye liken me, or shall I be equal? saith the Holy One" (Isa. 40:25), is God's own challenge. Thus, for any creature to deem himself "equal with God" would be the highest robbery and supremest blasphemy.

"But made Himself of no reputation." The meaning of the words is explained in those which immediately follow. So far was the Son from tenaciously insisting upon His personal rights as a member of the blessed Trinity, He voluntarily relinquished them. He willingly set aside the magnificent distinctions of the Creator, to appear in the form of a creature, yes, in the likeness of a fallen man. He abdicated His position of supremacy, and entered one of servitude. Though equal in majesty and glory with God, He joyfully resigned Himself to the Father's will (John 6:38). Incomparable condescension was this. He who was by inherent right in the form of God, suffered His glory to be eclipsed, His honor to be laid in the dust, and Himself to be humbled to a most shameful death.

"And took upon Him the form of a servant." In so doing, He did not cease to be all that He was before, but He assumed something He had not been previously. There was no change in His divine nature, but the uniting to His divine person of a human nature. "He who is God, can no more be not God, than he who is not God, can be God" (John Owen). None of Christ's divine attributes were relinquished, for they are as inseparable from His person as heat is from fire, or weight from substance. But His majestic glory was, for a season, obscured by the interposing veil of human flesh. Nor is this statement negated by John 1:14—"we beheld His glory" (explained by Matthew 16:17), in contrast from the unregenerate masses before whom He appeared as "a root out of a dry ground," having "no form nor comeliness" (Isa. 53:2).

It was God Himself who was "manifest in the flesh" (1 Tim. 3:16). The One born in Bethlehem's manger was "The mighty God" (Isa. 9:6), and heralded as, "Christ the Lord" (Luke 2:11). Let there be no uncertainty on this point. Had He been "emptied" of any of His personal excellency, had His divine attributes been laid aside, then His satisfaction or sacrifice would not have possessed infinite value. The glory of His person was not in the slightest degree diminished when He became incarnate, though it was (in measure) concealed by the lowly form of the servant He assumed. Christ was still "equal with God" when He descended to earth. It was "The Lord of glory" (1 Cor. 2:8) whom men crucified.

"And took upon Him the form of a servant." That was the great condescension, yet is it not possible for us to fully grasp the infinity of the Son's stoop. If God "humbleth Himself to behold the things that are in heaven, and in the earth!" (Ps. 113:6) how much more so to actually become "flesh" and be amongst the most lowly. He entered into an office which placed Him below God (John 14:28; 1 Corinthians 11:3). He was, for a season, "made lower than the angels" (Heb. 2:7); He was "made under the law" (Gal. 4:4). He was made lower than the ordinary condition of man, for He was "a reproach of men, and despised of the people" (Ps. 22:6).

What point all this gives to, "Let this mind be in you, which was also in Christ Jesus" (Phil. 2:5). How earnestly the Christian needs to seek grace to be content with the lowest place God and men assign him; to be ready to perform the meanest service; to be and do anything which brings glory to God.

CHAPTER 4
The Humanity of Christ

It has been truly said:

Right views concerning Christ are indispensable to a right faith, and a right faith is indispensable to salvation. To stumble at the foundation, is, concerning faith, to make shipwreck altogether; for as Immanuel, God with us, is the grand Object of faith, to err in views of His eternal Deity, or to err in views of His sacred humanity, is alike destructive. There are points of truth which are not fundamental, though erroneous views on any one point must lead to God-dishonoring consequences in strict proportion to its importance and magnitude; but there are certain foundation truths to err concerning which is to insure for the erroneous and the unbelieving, the blackness of darkness forever" (J. C. Philpot, 1859).

To know Christ as God, to know Him as man, to know Him as God-man, and this by a divine revelation of His person, is indeed to have eternal life in our hearts. Nor can He be known in any other way than by divine and special revelation. "But when it pleased God, who separated me from my mother's womb and called me by his grace, to reveal his Son in me" (Gal. 1:15-16). An imaginary conception of His person may be obtained by diligently studying the Scriptures, but a vital knowledge of Him must be communicated from on high (Matthew 16:17). A theoretical and theological knowledge of Christ is what the natural man may acquire, but a saving, soul-transforming view of Him (2 Cor. 3:18) is only given by the Spirit to the regenerate (1 John 5:20).

"But made himself of no reputation, and took upon him the form of a servant, and was made in the likeness of men" (Phil. 2:7). The first clause (and the preceding verse) was before us in the last two chapters. The two expressions we consider here balance with (and thus serve to explain) those in verse 6. The last clause of v. 7 is an exegesis of the one immediately preceding. "Made in the likeness of men" refers to the human nature Christ assumed. The "form of a servant" denotes the position or state which He entered. So, "equal with God" refers to the divine nature, the "form of God" signifies His manifested glory in His position of Lord over all.

The humanity of Christ was unique. History supplies no analogy, nor can His humanity be illustrated by anything in nature. It is incomparable, not only to our fallen human nature, but also to unfallen Adam's. The Lord Jesus was born into circumstances totally different from those in which Adam first found himself, but the sins and griefs of His people were on Him from the first. His humanity was produced neither by natural generation (as is ours), nor by special creation, as was Adam's. The humanity of Christ was, under the immediate agency of the Holy Spirit, supernaturally "conceived" (Isa. 7:14) of the virgin. It was "prepared" of God (Heb. 10:5); yet "made of a woman" (Gal. 4:4.).

The uniqueness of Christ's humanity also appears in that it never had a separate existence of its own. The eternal Son assumed (at the moment of Mary's conception) a human nature, but not a human person. This important distinction calls for careful consideration. By a "person" is meant an intelligent being subsisting by himself. The second person of the Trinity assumed a human nature and gave it subsistence by union with His divine personality. It would have been a human person, if it had not been united to the Son of God. But being united to Him, it cannot be called a person, because it never subsisted by itself, as other men do. Hence the force of "that holy thing which shall be born of thee" (Luke 1:35). It was not possible for a divine person to assume another person, subsisting of itself, into union with Himself. For two persons, remaining two, to become one person, is a contradiction. "A body hast thou prepared me" (Heb. 10:5). The "me" denotes the divine Person, the "body," the nature He took unto Himself.

The humanity of Christ was real. "Forasmuch then as the children are partakers of flesh and blood, he also Himself likewise took part of the same . . . Wherefore in all things it behoved him to be made like unto his brethren" (Heb. 2:14, 17). He assumed a complete human nature, spirit, soul, and body. Christ did not bring His human nature from heaven (as some have strangely and erroneously concluded from 1 Corinthians 15:47), but it was composed of the very substance of His mother. In clothing Himself with flesh and blood, Christ also clothed Himself with human feelings, so He did not differ from His brethren, sin only excepted.

"While we always contend that Christ is God, let us never lose the conviction He is most certainly a man. He is not God humanized, nor a human deified; but, as to His Godhead, pure Godhead, equal and coeternal with the Father; as to His manhood, perfect manhood, made in all respects like the rest of mankind, sin alone excepted. His humanity is real, for He was born. He lay in the virgin's womb, and in due time was born. The gate by which we enter our first life he passed through also. He was not created, nor transformed, but His humanity was begotten and born. As He was born, so in the circumstances of His birth, he is completely human. He was as weak and feeble as any other babe. He is not even royal, but human. Those born in marble halls of old were wrapped in purple garments, and were thought by the common people to be a superior race. But this Babe was wrapped in swaddling clothes and had a manger for a cradle, so that the true humanity of His being would come out."

As He grows up, the very growth shows how completely human He is. He does not spring into full manhood at once, but He grows in wisdom and stature, and in favor with God and man. When he reaches man's estate, He gets the common stamp of manhood upon His brow. "In the sweat of thy brow shalt thou eat bread" is the common heritage of us all, and He receives no better. The carpenter's shop must witness to the toils of a Savior, and when He becomes the preacher and the prophet, still we read such significant words as these—"Jesus, being weary sat thus on the well." We find Him needing to betake Himself to rest in sleep. He slumbers at the stem of the vessel when it is tossed in the midst of the tempest. Brethren, if sorrow be the mark of real manhood, and "man is born unto trouble as the sparks fly upward," certainly Jesus Christ has the truest evidence of being a man. If to hunger and to thirst be signs that He was no shadow, and His manhood no fiction, you have these. If to associate with His fellow-men, and eat and drink as they did, will be proof to your mind that He was none other than a man, you see Him sitting at a feast one day, at another time He graces a marriage-supper, and on another occasion He is hungry and "hath not where to lay His head" (C. H. Spurgeon).

They who deny Christ's derivation of real humanity through His mother undermine the atonement. His very fraternity (Heb. 2:11), as our Kinsman-Redeemer, depended on the fact that He obtained His humanity from Mary. Without this He would neither possess the natural nor the legal union with His people, which must lie at the foundation of His representative character as the "last Adam." To be our Goel (Redeemer), His humanity could neither be brought from heaven nor immediately created by God, but must be derived, as ours was, from a human mother. But with this difference: His humanity never existed in Adam's covenant to entail guilt or taint.

The humanity of Christ was holy. Intrinsically so, because it was "of the Holy Ghost" (Matthew 1:20); absolutely so, because taken into union with God, the Holy One. This fact is expressly affirmed in Luke 1:35, "that holy thing," which is contrasted with, "but we are all as an unclean thing" (Isa. 64:6), and that because we are "shapen in iniquity" and conceived "in sin" (Ps. 51:5). Though Christ truly became partaker of our nature, yet He was "holy, harmless, undefiled, separate from sinners" (Heb. 7:26). For this reason He could say, "For the prince of this world cometh, and hath nothing in me" (John 14:30). There was nothing in His pure humanity which could respond to sin or Satan.

It was truly remarkable when man was made in the image of God (Gen. 1:26). But bow in wonderment and worship at the amazing condescension of God being made in the image of man! How this manifests the greatness of His love and the riches of His grace! It was for His people and their salvation that the eternal Son assumed human nature and abased Himself even to death. He drew a veil over His glory that He might remove our reproach. Surely, pride must be forever renounced by the followers of such a Savior.

Inasmuch as "the man Christ Jesus" (1 Tim. 2:5) lived in this world for thirty-three years, He has left "an example, that ye should follow his steps" (1 Peter 2:21). He "did no sin," nor should we (1 Cor. 15:24). "Neither was guile found in his mouth," nor should it be in ours (Col. 4:6). "When he was reviled, He reviled not again," nor must His followers. He was weary in body, but not in well-doing. He suffered hunger and thirst, yet never murmured. He "pleased not himself" (Rom. 15:3), nor must we (2 Cor. 5:15). He always did those things which pleased the Father (John 8:29). This too must ever be our aim (2 Cor. 5:9).

CHAPTER 5
The Person of Christ

We enter with fear and trembling upon this high and holy subject. Christ's name is called "Wonderful" (Isa. 9:6), and even the angels of God are commanded to worship Him (Heb. 1:6). There is no salvation apart from a true knowledge of Him (John 17:3). "Whosoever denieth the Son [either His true Godhead, or His true and holy humanity] . . . hath not the Father" (1 John 2:23). They are thrice-blessed to whom the Spirit of Truth communicates a supernatural revelation of the Being of Christ (Matthew 16:17). It will lead them in the only path of wisdom and joy, for in Him "are hid all the treasures of wisdom and knowledge" (Col. 2:3) until they are taken to be where He is and behold His supernal glory forever (John 17:24). An increasing apprehension of the Truth concerning the person of Christ should be our constant aim.

"Without controversy great is the mystery of godliness: God was manifest in the flesh" (1 Tim. 3:16). In view of such a divine declaration as this, it is both useless and impious for any man to attempt an explanation of the wondrous and unique person of the Lord Jesus. He cannot be fully comprehended by any finite intelligence. "No man knoweth the Son, but the Father" (Matthew 11:27). Nevertheless, it is our privilege to grow "in the knowledge of our Lord and Savior Jesus Christ" (2 Pet. 3:18). So too it is the duty of His servants to hold up the person of the God-man as revealed in Holy Scriptures, as well as to warn against errors which cloud His glory.

The one born in Bethlehem's manger was "the mighty God" (Isa. 9:6), "Immanuel" (Matthew 1:23), "the great God and our Savior" (Titus 2:13). He is also the true Man, with a spirit, a soul and a body, for these are essential to human nature. None could be real man without all three. Nevertheless, the humanity of Christ (that holy thing, Luke 1:35) is not a distinct person, separate from His Godhead, for it never had a separate existence before taken into union with His deity. He is the God-man, yet "one Lord" (Eph. 4:5). As such He was born, lived here in this world, died, rose again, ascended to heaven, and will continue thus for all eternity. As such He is entirely unique, and the Object of lasting wonder to all holy beings.

The person of Christ is a composite one. Two separate natures are united in one peerless Person; but they are not fused into each other, instead, they remain distinct and different. The human nature is not divine, nor has it been, intrinsically, deified, for it possesses none of the attributes of God. The humanity of Christ, absolutely and separately considered, is neither omnipotent, omniscient, nor omnipresent. On the other hand, His deity is not a creature, and has none of the properties which pertain to such. Taking to Himself a human nature did not effect any change in His divine being. It was a divine person who wedded to Himself a holy humanity, and though His essential glory was partly veiled, yet it never ceased to be, nor did His divine attributes cease to function. As the God-man, Christ is the "one mediator" (1 Tim. 2:5). He alone was fitted to stand between God and men and effect a reconciliation between them.

It needs to be maintained that the two natures are united in the one person of Christ, but that each retains its separate properties, just as the soul and body of men do, though united. Thus, in His divine nature, Christ has nothing in common with us—nothing finite, derived or dependent. But in His human nature, He was made in all things like to His brethren, sin excepted. In that nature He was born in time, and did not exist from all eternity. He increased in knowledge and other endowments. In the one nature He had a comprehensive knowledge of all things; in the other, He knew nothing but by communication or derivation. In the one nature He had an infinite and sovereign will; in the other, He had a creature will. Though not opposed to the divine will, its conformity to it was of the same kind with that in perfect creatures.

The necessity for the two natures in the one person of our Savior is self-evident. It was fitting that the Mediator should be both God and man, that He might partake of the nature of both parties and be a middle person between them, filling up the distance and bringing them near to each other. Only thus was He able to communicate His benefits to us; and only thus could He discharge our obligations. As Witsius, the Dutch theologian (1690) pointed out: "None but God could restore us to true liberty. If any creature could redeem us we should be the peculiar property of that creature: but it is a manifest contradiction to be free and yet at the same time be the servant of any creature. So too none but God could give us eternal life: hence the two are joined together—'The true God, and eternal life' (1 John 5:20)."

It was equally necessary that the Mediator be Man. He was to enter our Law-place, be subject to the Law, keep it, and merit by keeping it. "But when the fullness of the time was come, God sent forth His Son, made of a woman, made under the law" (Gal. 4:4). Note the order. He must first be "made of a woman," before He could be "made under the law." But more, He had to endure the curse of the Law, suffer its penalty. He was to be "made sin" for His people, and the wages of sin is death. But that was impossible to Him until He took upon Him a nature capable of mortality. "Forasmuch then as the children are partakers of flesh and blood, He also himself likewise took part of the same; that through death he might destroy him that had the power of death, that is, the devil" (Heb. 2:14).

Thus, the person of the God-man is unique. His birth had no precedent and His existence no analogy. He cannot be explained by referring Him to a class, nor can He be illustrated by an example. The Scriptures, while fully revealing all the elements of His person, yet never present in one formula an exhaustive definition of that person, nor a connected statement of the elements which constitute it and their mutual relationships. The "mystery" is indeed great. How is it possible that the same person should be at the same time infinite and finite, omnipotent and helpless? He altogether transcends our understanding. How can two complete spirits coalesce in one person? How can two consciousnesses, two understandings, two memories, two wills, constitute one person? No one can explain it. Nor are we called upon to do so. Both natures act in concert in one person. All the attributes and acts of both natures are referred to one person. The same person who gave His life for the sheep, possessed glory with the Father before the world was!

This amazing Personality does not center in His humanity, nor is it a compound one originated by the power of the Holy Spirit when He brought those two natures together in the womb of the virgin Mary. It was not by adding manhood to Godhead that His personality was formed. The Trinity is eternal and unchangeable. A new person is not substituted for the second member of the Trinity; neither is a fourth added. The person of Christ is just the eternal Word, who in time, by the power of the Holy Spirit, through the instrument of the virgin's womb, took a human nature (not at that time a man, but the seed of Abraham) into personal union with Himself. The Person is eternal and divine; His humanity was introduced into it. The center of His personality is always in the eternal and personal Word, or Son of God.

Though no analogy exists by which we may illustrate the mysterious person of Christ, there is a most remarkable type in Exodus 3:2-6. The "flame of fire" in the midst of the "bush," was an emblem of the presence of God indwelling the Man Christ Jesus. Observe that the One who appeared there to Moses is termed, first, "the angel of the LORD," which declares the relation of Christ to the Father, namely, "the angel (messenger) of the covenant." But secondly, this angel said unto Moses, "I am the God of Abraham," that is what He was absolutely in Himself. The fire—emblem of Him who is a "consuming fire"—placed itself in a bush (a thing of the earth), where it burned, yet the bush was not consumed. A remarkable foreshadowing this was of the "fullness of the Godhead," dwelling in Christ (Col. 2:9). That this is the meaning of the type is clear, when we read of "The good will of him that dwelt in the bush" (Deut. 33:16).

The great mystery of the Trinity is that one Spirit should subsist eternally as three distinct Persons: the mystery of the person of Christ is that two separate spirits (divine and human) should constitute but one person. The moment we deny the unity of His person we enter the bogs of error. Christ is the God-man. The humanity of Christ was not absorbed by His deity, but preserves its own characteristics. Scripture does not hesitate to say, "Jesus increased in wisdom and stature, and in favor with God and man" (Luke 2:52). Christ is both infinite and finite, self-sufficient and dependent at the same time, because His Person embraces, two different natures, the divine and the human.

In the incarnation the second Person of the Trinity established a personal union between Himself and a human spirit, soul, and body. His two natures remained and remain distinct, and their properties or active powers are inseparable from each nature respectively.

The union between them is not mechanical, as that between oxygen and nitrogen in our air; neither is it chemical, as between oxygen and hydrogen when water is formed; neither is it organic, as that subsisting between our hearts and brains; but it is a union more intimate, more profound, and more mysterious than any of these. It is personal. If we cannot understand the nature of the simpler unions, why should we complain because we cannot understand the nature of the most profound of all unions? (A. A. Hodge, to whom we are also indebted for a number of other thoughts in this article).

"Is there a thing beneath the sun
That strives with Thee my heart to share?

O tear it thence, and reign alone,
The Lord of every motion there.
Then shall my heart from earth be free,
When it has found repose in Thee.

CHAPTER 6
The Subsistence of Christ

The ground we now tread upon is quite unknown even to the majority of God's people (so great has been the spiritual and theological deterioration of the last century—though it was familiar to the better-taught saints of the Puritans' times and of those who followed. That the Son of God is coequal with the Father and the Spirit, and that nearly 2,000 years ago the Word became flesh and was made in the likeness of men, is still held firmly (and will be) by all truly regenerated souls. That it is the union of the divine and human natures in His wondrous person which fits Him for His mediatorial office, is also apprehended more or less clearly. But that is about as far as the light of nearly all Christians can take them. That the God-man subsisted in heaven before the world was is a blessed truth which has been lost to the last few generations.

A thoughtful reader who ponders a verse such as John 6:62 must surely be puzzled. "What and if ye shall see the Son of man ascend up where he was before?" Mark it well that our Redeemer there spoke of Himself not as the Son before He became incarnate. But ignorant as we may be of this precious truth, Old Testament saints were instructed therein, as evident from Psalm 80, where Asaph prays, "Let thy hand be upon the man of thy right hand, upon the son of man whom thou madest strong for thyself" (v. 17). Yes, the Man Christ Jesus, taken into union with Himself by the second person of the Trinity, subsisted before the Father from all eternity, and was the object of the Old Testament saints' faith.

When first presented, the last statement appears to be mysticism run wild, or downright heresy. It would be if we had said that the soul and body of the Son of Man had any existence before He was born at Bethlehem. But this is not what Scripture teaches. What the written Word affirms is that the Mediator (Christ in His two natures) had a real subsistence before God from all eternity. First, He was "foreordained before the foundation of the world" (1 Pet. 1:20). He was chosen by God to be the Head of the whole election of grace (see Isaiah 42:1). But more; it was not only purposed by God that the Mediator (the Man Christ Jesus wedded to the eternal Word, John 1:1, 14) should have an historical existence when the "fullness of time" (Gal. 4:4) had arrived, but He had an actual subsistence before Him long before that. But how could this be?

In seeking the answer, it will help us to contemplate something which, though not strictly analogous, on a lower plane serves to illustrate the principle. Hebrews 11:1 records that "faith is the substance of things hoped for." The Greek word for "substance" more properly signifies "a real subsistence." It is opposed to what is only an image of the imagination, it is the antithesis of fantasy. Faith gives a real subsistence in the mind and heart of things which are yet to be, so that they are enjoyed now and their power is experienced in the soul. Faith lays hold of the things God has promised so that they become actually present.

If faith possesses the power to add reality to what as yet has no historical actuality; if faith can enjoy in the present that whose existence is yet future, how much more was God able to give the Mediator a covenant subsistence endless ages before He was born. In consequence, Christ was the Son of Man in heaven, secretly before God, before He became the Son of Man openly in this world. As Christ declared of His Father in the language of prophecy, "In the shadow of his hand hath he hid me, and made me a polished shaft: in his quiver hath he hid me (Isa. 49:2). Note that the verses which follow refer to the everlasting covenant. The "quiver" of God is a fine expression to denote the secrecy and security in which the purpose of God was concealed.

Many passages speak of this wondrous subject. Perhaps the clearest, and the one with the most detail, is Proverbs 8. The term "wisdom" (v. 12) is one of the names of Christ (see 1 Corinthians 1:24). That "wisdom" has reference to a person is clear (v. 17), and to a divine person (v. 15). The whole passage (vv. 13-36) has Christ in view, but in what character has not been clearly discerned. While it is evident that what is said (vv. 15-16, 32-36) could only apply to a divine person, it should be equally plain that some of the terms (vv. 23-24 ff.) cannot be predicated of the Son of God. Contemplated only as coeternal and coequal with the Father, it could not be said that Christ was ever "brought forth."

From all the terms used in Proverbs 8:13-36 it should be apparent that some are impossible to understand of Christ's deity (separately considered), as others of them cannot be of His humanity only. But the difficulties disappear once we see that the whole passage contemplates the Mediator, the God-man in His two natures. The Man Christ Jesus, as united to the second Person of the Godhead, was "possessed" (v. 22), by the Triune God from all eternity. Let us note some things about this marvelous passage: "The Lord possessed me in the beginning of his way, before his works of old" (v. 22). The speaker is the Mediator, who had a covenant subsistence before God ere the universe came into being. The Man Christ Jesus, taken into union with the eternal Son, was "the beginning" of the Triune God's "way." It is difficult to speak of eternal matters as first, second, and third, yet God set them forth in the Scriptures for us, and it is permissible to use such distinctions to aid our understanding. The first act or counsel of God had respect to the Man Christ Jesus. He was appointed to be not only the Head of His Church, but also "the firstborn of all creation" (Col. 1:15). The predestination of the Man Christ Jesus unto the grace of divine union and glory was the first of God's decrees: "in the head [Gr.] of the book" it was written of him (Heb. 10:7; cf. Isa. 42:1; Rev. 13:8).

The person of the God-man Mediator was the foundation of all the divine counsels (cf. Ephesians 3:11; 1:9-10). He was ordained to be the cornerstone, on which all creation was to rest. As such, the Triune Jehovah "possessed" or "embraced" Him as a treasury in which all the divine counsels were laid up, as an efficient Agent for the execution of all His works. As such, He is both "the wisdom of God" and "the power of God" executively, being a perfect vehicle through which to express Himself. As such, He was "the beginning" of God's way. The "way" of God, signifies the outworking of His eternal decrees, the accomplishing of His purposes by wise and holy dispensations (cf. Isaiah 55:8-9).

"I was set up from everlasting" (v. 23). This could not be spoken of the Son Himself, for as God He was not capable of being "set up." Yet how could He be set up as the God-man Mediator? By mediatorial settlement, by covenant-constitution, by divine subsistence before the mind of God. From the womb of eternity, in the "counsel of peace" (Zech. 6:13), before all worlds, Jesus Christ was in His official character "set up." Before God planned to create any creature, He first set up Christ as the great Archetype and Original. There was an order in God's counsels as well as creation, and Christ has "the pre-eminence" in all things.

The Hebrew verb for "set up" is "anointed," and should have been so translated. The reference is to the appointing and investing of Christ with the mediatorial office, which was done in the everlasting covenant. All the glory our Lord possesses as Mediator was then granted to Him, on the condition of His obedience and sufferings. Therefore when He finished His work He prayed, "Glorify thou me with thine own self with the glory which I had with thee before the world was" (John 17:5). The glory which is there expressly in view is that exalted place which had been given to Him as the Head of all creation. In the timeless transactions of the everlasting covenant, in the unique honor which had been accorded Him as the "Beginning" of God's "way," the "firstborn of all creation," He had this glory. For the open manifestation of it He now prayed—answered at His ascension.

"When there were no depths, I was brought forth" (v 24). "Brought forth" out of the womb of God's decrees; "brought forth" into covenant-subsistence before the divine mind; "brought forth" as the Image of the invisible God; "brought forth" as the Man Christ Jesus, after whose likeness Adam was created. Though Adam was the first man by open manifestation on earth, Christ had the priority as He secretly subsisted in heaven. Adam was created in the image and after the likeness of Christ as He actually, but secretly, subsisted in the person of the Son of God, who, in the fullness of time, was born openly.

"Then I was by him, as one brought up with him" (v. 30). Gesenius says that the Hebrew verb here is connected with one which means "to prop, stay, sustain," and hence "such as one may safely lean on." It is rendered "nurse" in Ruth 4:16 and 2 Samuel 4:4. As men commit their children to a nurse to cherish and train, so God committed His counsels to Christ. The Hebrew word for "brought up" also signifies a "master-builder" (RV). Christ took the fabric of the universe upon Himself, to contrive the framing of it with the most exquisite skill. It is akin to the Hebrew word "amen," which has the same letters as the verb to which Gesenius refers, only with different vowel points. How blessedly it describes Him who could be relied upon to carry out the Father's purpose!

"And I was daily his delight, rejoicing always before him" (v 30). It is not absolutely the mutual eternal delight of the Father and the Son, arising from the perfection of the same Divine excellency in each person that is intended. But respect is plainly had unto the counsels of God concerning the salvation of mankind by Him who is His "Wisdom" and "Power" unto that end. The counsel of "peace" was between Jehovah and the Branch (Zech. 6:13), or the Father and the Son as He was to become incarnate. For therein was He "foreordained before the foundation of the world" (1 Pet. 1:20) namely, to be a Savior and Deliverer, by whom all the counsels of God were to be accomplished, and this by His own will and concurrence with the Father. And such a foundation was laid of the salvation of the Church in those counsels of God, as transacted between the Father and the Son, that it is said (Titus 1:2), "eternal life" was "promised before the world began" (J. Owen).

CHAPTER 7
The Servitude of Christ

God has many servants, not only on earth, but also in heaven. The angels are "all ministering spirits" (Heb. 1:14) who, "do his commandments, hearkening unto the voice of his word" (Ps. 103:20). But what we now contemplate is not any servant of God or from God, but something infinitely more blessed and amazing, the Divine Servant Himself. What a remarkable phenomenon, an anomaly in any other connection. Yes, what amounts to a contradiction in terms, for supremacy and subordination, Godhood and servanthood, are opposites. Yet this is the surprising conjunction Holy Writ sets before us: that the Most High abased Himself, the Lord of glory assumed the form of a menial, the King of kings became a subject. Most of us at least were taught from childhood that the Son of God took unto Himself our nature and was born as a Babe at Bethlehem. Perhaps our familiarity with this tended to blunt our sense of wonderment at it. Let us ponder not so much the miracle or mystery of the Divine Incarnation, but the fact itself.

"Behold, my servant shall deal prudently, he shall be exalted and extolled, and be very high" (Isa. 52:13). There are four things here: First, the note of exclamation, "Behold"; Second, the subject, the divine "servant"; Third, the perfection of His work, "shall deal prudently"; Fourth, the reward bestowed upon Him, "He shall be exalted and extolled." The opening "behold" is not only a call for us to focus our gaze upon and adoringly consider the One before us, but also and primarily as an exclamation or note of wonderment. What an amazing spectacle to see the Maker of heaven and earth in the form of a Servant, the Giver of the Law Himself become subject to it. What an astonishing phenomenon that the Lord of Glory should take upon Him such an office. How this ought to stir our souls. "Behold!" wonder at it, be filled with holy awe, and then consider what our response ought to be.

"Behold, my servant." None other than the Father Himself owns Christ in this office. This is most blessed, for it is in sharp contrast from the treatment He received at the hands of men. It was because the Messiah appeared in servant form that the Jews despised and rejected Him. "Is not this the carpenter, the son of Mary . . . And they were offended at him" (Mark 6:3). Apparently the holy angels were nonplussed at such an incredible sight, for they received, and needed, the divine order, "Let all the angels of God worship him" when He brought His firstbegotten into the world (Heb. 1:6). "Let," as though they were uncertain, as well they might be now that their Maker had assumed creature form; "all the angels of God," none excepted, the highest as well as the lowest, archangel, cherubim, seraphim, principalities, and powers; "worship him," render homage and praise unto Him, for far from His self-abasement having tarnished His personal glory, it enhanced it.

How blessed to hear the Father testifying of His approbation of the One who had entered Bethlehem's manger, bidding the angels not to be staggered by so unparalleled a sight, but to continue worshiping the second Person in the Holy Trinity even though He now wore a menial garb. Nor has the Holy Spirit failed to record their obedience, for He has told us that while the shepherds were keeping watch over their flock by night, a celestial messenger announced the Savior's birth, "And suddenly there was with the angel a multitude of the heavenly host praising God, and saying, Glory to God in the highest, and on earth peace, good will toward men" (Luke 2:13-14). How jealous the Father was of His incarnate Son's honor! It was evidenced again when He condescended to be baptized in the Jordan, for "The heavens were opened unto him," the Spirit of God descended like a dove and abode upon Him, and the Father declared, "This is my beloved Son, in whom I am well pleased" (Matthew 3:16-17). "Behold, my servant" He says to us.

"Shall deal prudently." Here we need to be on our guard, lest we interpret carnally. In the judgment of the world, to "deal prudently" is to act tactfully. Nine times out of ten tact is nothing more than a compromise of principle. Measured by the standards of unregenerate "policy," Christ acted very imprudently. He could have spared Himself much suffering had He been "less extreme" and followed the religious tide of His day. He could have avoided much opposition had He been milder in His denunciations of the Pharisees or withheld those aspects of the truth which are most distasteful to the natural man. Had He been more tactful as this evil generation considers things, He had never overthrown the tables of the moneychangers in the temple and charged such unholy traffickers with making His Father's house "a den of thieves," for it was then He began to "make so much trouble for Himself." But from the spiritual viewpoint, from the angle of ever having the Father's glory in view, from the side of seeking the eternal good of His own, Christ ever "dealt prudently." None other than the Father testifies to the fact.

Instead of illustrating where Christ dealt "prudently," we have sought to dispose of a general misconception and warn against interpreting that expression in a fleshly manner, it is true the Christian may, in rashness or acting with a zeal that is not according to knowledge, bring upon himself much unnecessary trouble; yet if he is faithful to God and uncompromising in his separation from the world, he is certain to incur the hatred and opposition of the ungodly. He must expect religious professors to tell him he has only himself to blame, that his lack of tact has made things so unpleasant for him. Christ's dealing prudently means He acted wisely. He never erred, never acted foolishly, never did anything which needed to be corrected; but the wisdom from which He acted was not of this world, but was "from above," and therefore was "pure, then peaceable, gentle" (James 3:17). O for more of such prudence—obtained by communion with Christ, drinking in of His Spirit.

"He shall be exalted and extolled and be very high." This tells of the reward given Christ for His willingness to become a "servant" and for His faithfulness in discharging that office. It tells us first of the Father's own valuation of His Son's condescension and of the recompense He has made the One who became obedient unto death. "Wherefore God hath highly exalted him. and given him a name which is above every name: that at the name of Jesus every knee should bow, of things in heaven, and things in earth, and things under the earth; and that every tongue should confess that Jesus Christ is Lord to the glory of God the Father" (Phil. 2:9-11). The perfect Servant has been exalted to the Throne, seated "on the right hand of the Majesty on high" (Heb. 1:3), "angels and authorities and powers being made subject unto him" (1 Pet. 3:22). It tells also of Christ's exaltation in the affections of His people. Nothing endears the Redeemer more to their hearts than the realization that it was for their sakes He "became poor" and abased Himself. "Worthy is the Lamb that was slain to receive power, and riches, and wisdom, and strength, and honor, and glory, and blessing" (Rev. 5:12) is their united testimony.

CHAPTER 8
The Despisement of Christ

"He is despised and rejected of men" (Isa. 53:3), forms part one of the
Messianic predictions. God made known long beforehand the treatment His
Son would receive when He became incarnate. The prophecy of Isaiah was
in the hands of the Jews 700 years before Jesus was born at Bethlehem; yet,
so exactly did it describe what befell Him that it might well have been
written by one of the apostles. Here is one of the incontrovertible proofs of
the divine inspiration of Scriptures, for only One who knew the end from the
beginning could have written this history beforehand.

It might have been supposed that the coming to earth of the Lord of glory
would meet with a warm welcome and reverent reception; and more so in
view of His appearing in human form, and His going about doing good.
Since He came not to judge, but to save, since His mission was one of grace
and mercy, since He ministered to the needy and healed the sick, will not
men gladly receive Him? Many would naturally think so, but in so doing
they overlook the fact that the Lord Jesus is "the Holy One." None but those
who have the principle of holiness in their hearts can appreciate ineffable
Purity. Such an assumption as just mentioned ignores the solemn fact of
human depravity: the heart of fallen man is "desperately wicked" (Jer. 17:9).
How can the Holy One appear attractive to those who are full of sin!

Nothing so clearly evidences the condition of the human heart, nor so
solemnly demonstrates its corruption, as its attitude toward Christ. Much is
recorded against man in the Old Testament (see Psalm 14:1-4); yet, dark as
its picture is of fallen human nature, it fades into insignificance before what
the New Testament sets before us. "The carnal mind is enmity against God"
(Rom. 8:7); never was this so frightfully patent as when He was manifested
in flesh. "If I had not come, and spoken unto them, they had not had sin: but
now they have no cloke for their sin" (John 15:22). The appearing of Christ
fully exposed man, and brings to light as nothing else has the desperate
wickedness of his heart. Let us consider three questions: Who was (and still

is) "despised and rejected of men"? Why is He so grievously slighted? In what way is He scorned?

Who was so unwelcome here? First, the One who pressed upon men the absolute sovereignty of God. Few things are so distasteful to the proud human heart as the truth that God does as He pleases, without consulting with the creature; that He dispenses His favors entirely according to His imperial will. Fallen man has no claims upon Him, is destitute of any merit, and can do nothing whatever to win God's esteem. Fallen man is a spiritual pauper, entirely dependent upon divine charity. In bestowing His mercies, God is regulated by nothing but His own "good pleasure." "Is it not lawful for me to do what I will with mine own?" (Matthew 20:15) is His unanswerable challenge; yet, as the context shows, man wickedly murmurs against this.

The Lord Jesus came to glorify His Father, therefore we find Him maintaining His crown-rights and emphasizing His sovereignty. In His First message, in the Capernaum synagogue, He pointed out there were many widows in Israel during the days of Elijah. But when there was great famine throughout the land, the prophet was not sent to any but one at Zarephath; and though there were many lepers in Israel in the time of Elisha, none were healed, except by distinguishing mercy shown to Naaman, the Syrian. The sequel was, "All they in the synagogue, when they heard these things, were filled with wrath, and rose up and thrust him out of the city, and led him unto the brow of the hill whereon their city was built, that they might cast him down headlong" (Luke 4:28-29). For pressing the truth of God's absolute sovereignty, Christ was "despised and rejected of men."

Who was so unwelcome here? Second, the One who upheld God's Law. In it is the divine authority expressed, and complete subjection to it is required from the creature: thus Christ pressed the demands of God's Law upon man. "Think not that I am come to destroy the law, or the prophets: I am not come to destroy, but to fulfill" (Matthew 5:17); "All things whatsoever ye would that men should do to you, do ye even so to them: for this is the law and the prophets" (Matthew 7:12). But fallen men resent restraints, and want to be a law unto themselves. Their language concerning God and His Christ is, "Let us break their bands asunder and cast away their cords from us" (Ps. 2:3). Because the Lord Jesus enforced the requirements of the Decalogue He was "despised and rejected of men." A solemn illustration of this occurs when he spoke to the Jews, "Did not Moses give you the law, and yet none of you keepeth the law. Why go ye about to kill me?" (John 7:19). What was their response? "The people answered and said, Thou hast a devil" (v. 20).

Who was so unwelcome here? Third, the One who denounced human tradition in the religious sphere. Despite the fall, man is essentially a religious creature. The image of God in which he was originally created has not been completely destroyed. The world over, blacks and whites, reds and yellows, pay homage to gods of their own devising; there are few things on which they are more tender than their sacerdotal superstitions. He who condemns, or even criticizes, the devotees of any form or order of worship, will be greatly disliked. Christ drew upon Himself the hatred of Israel's leaders by His denunciation of their inventions. He charged them with "making the Word of God of none effect through their tradition" (Mark 7:13). When He cleansed the temple, the chief priests and scribes were "sore displeased" (Matthew 21:15).

Who was so unwelcome here? Fourth, the One who repudiated an empty profession. Nothing so infuriated the Jews as Christ's exposure and denunciation of their vain pretensions. Since He was omniscient, it was impossible to impose upon Him; inflexibly righteous, He could not accept deceptions; absolutely holy, He must insist upon sincerity and reality. When they declared "Abraham is our father," He answered, "If ye were Abraham's children, ye would do the works of Abraham." When they added, "we have one Father, even God," He replied, "If God were your Father, ye would love me . . . ye are of your father, the devil, and the lusts of your father ye will do." This so riled them that they exclaimed, "Say we not well that thou are a Samaritan, and hast a devil" (John 8:48).

On another occasion, the Jews asked Him, "How long dost thou make us to doubt? If thou be the Christ, tell us plainly" (John 10:24). He at once exposed their hypocrisy by saying, "I told you, and ye believed not . . . But ye believe not, because ye are not of my sheep . . . My sheep hear my voice, and I know them, and they follow me" (John 10:25-27). They were so angry they "took stones again to stone him." Men will not tolerate One who pierces their religious disguise, exposes their shams, and repudiates their fair but empty profession. It is the same today.

Who was so unwelcome here? Fifth, the One who exposed and denounced sin. This explains why Christ was not wanted here. He was a constant thorn in their sides. His holiness condemned their unholiness. Men wish to go their own way, to please themselves, to gratify their lusts. They want to be comfortable in their wickedness, therefore they resent that which searches the heart, pierces the conscience, rebukes their evil. Christ was absolutely uncompromising. He would not wink at wrongdoing, but unsparingly denounced it, in whomever He found it. He boldly affirmed, "For judgment I am come into this world" i.e., to discover men's secret characters, to prove they are blind in spiritual things, to demonstrate they love darkness rather than light. His person and preaching tested everything and everyone with whom He came into contact.

Why was (and is) Christ "despised and rejected of men?" First, because He required inward purity. Here is the great difference between all human religions and divine: the former concern themselves with external performances; the latter with the source of all conduct. "Man looketh on the outward appearance, but the LORD looketh on the heart" (1 Sam. 16:7). Christ's exposition and enforcement of this truth made Him unpopular with the leaders.

Woe unto you, scribes and Pharisees, hypocrites! for ye make clean the outside of the cup and of the platter, but within they are full of extortion and excess. Thou blind Pharisee, cleanse first that which is within the cup and platter, that the outside of them may be clean also. Woe unto you, scribes and Pharisees, hypocrites! for ye are like unto whited sepulchres, which indeed appear beautiful outward, but are within full of dead men's bones, and of all uncleanness. Even so ye also outwardly appear righteous unto men, but within ye are full of hypocrisy and iniquity" (Matthew 23:25-28).

Why was Christ "despised and rejected of men?" Second, because He demanded repentance. "Repent ye, and believe the gospel" (Mark 1:15), was His demanding call. That order is unchanging, for it is impossible to believe the Gospel till the heart be contrite. Repentance is taking sides with God against ourselves. It is the unsparing judgment of ourselves because of our high-handed rebellion. It is a ceasing to love and tolerate sin, and to excuse ourselves for committing it. It is a mourning before God because of our transgressions of His holy Law. Therefore, Christ taught, "Except ye repent, ye shall all likewise perish" (Luke 13:3), for He would not condone evil. He came to save His people from their sins, and not in them.

Why was Christ "despised and rejected of men?"

Third, because He insisted on the denial of self. This is on two principal points, namely, indulging and exalting of self. All fleshly lusts are to be unsparingly mortified, and self-righteousness is allowed no place in the gospel scheme. This was unmistakably plain in our Lord's teaching: "If any man will come after me, let him deny himself, and take up his cross, and follow me" (Matthew 16:24). Yet nothing is more contrary to the desires of the natural man, and Christ's insistence upon these terms of discipleship causes Him to be despised and rejected of men.

How is Christ "despised and rejected of men?" In different ways, and in varying degrees: professedly and practically, in words and in works. It is most important to clearly recognize this, for Satan deceives a great many souls at this point. He deludes them into supposing that because they are not guilty of what pertains to the avowed infidel and blatant atheist, therefore they are innocent of the fearful sin of slighting and defying the Lord Jesus. My reader, the solemn fact remains that there are millions of people in Christendom who, though not atheists and infidels, yet despise and reject the Christ of God. "They profess that they know God; but in works they deny him, being abominable, and disobedient, and unto every good work reprobate" (Titus 1:16). That verse clearly enunciates the principle.

Christ's authority is "despised" by those who disregard His precepts and commandments. Christ's yoke is "rejected" by those who are determined to be lord over themselves. Christ's glory is "despised" by those who bear His name yet have no concern whether their walk honors Him or no. Christ's Gospel is "rejected" by those who on the one hand affirm that sinners may be saved without repenting of and turning away from their sins, and on the other hand by those who teach heaven may be won by our own good works.

There are some who intellectually reject Christ, by repudiating His claims, denying that He is God the Son, assumed a holy and impeccable humanity, and died a vicarious death to save His people from their sins. Others virtually and practically reject Christ. There are those who profess to believe in the existence of God, own His power, and talk about His wondrous handiwork; yet they have not His fear upon them and are not in subjection to Him. So there are many who claim to trust in the finished work of Christ, yet their daily walk is no different from that of thousands of respectable worldlings. They profess to be Christians; yet are covetous, unscrupulous, untruthful, proud, self-willed, uncharitable; in a word, utterly unchristian.

CHAPTER 9
The Crucifixion of Christ

"They crucified Him . . . and sitting down they watched Him there" (Matthew 27:35-36). The reference is to Roman soldiers, as is clear from John 19:23, and confirmed by Matthew 27:54. They were authorized to carry out the death sentence passed by Pilate, and into their hands the governor had delivered the Savior (vv. 26-27). With coarse scurrility they executed the task. Adding insult to injury, they exposed the Lord Jesus to the indignities of a mock coronation: robing Him in scarlet, crowning Him with thorns, hailing Him as King of the Jews. Giving full expression to their enmity, they spat upon Him, smote Him with a reed, and mocked Him. Restoring to Him His raiment, they conducted Him to Golgotha and affixed Him to the cross. Having gambled for His garments, they sat down to watch Him to frustrate any attempt at rescue His friends might make, and to wait until life was extinct. Let us note three things:

First, the circumstances. The religious leaders of Israel had taken the initiative, for there "assembled together the chief priests, and the scribes, and the elders of the people, unto the palace of the high priest, who was called Caiaphas. And consulted that they might take Jesus by subtilty, and kill him" (Matthew 26:3-4). How many of the foulest crimes which have blackened the pages of history were perpetrated by ecclesiastical dignitaries. Yet the common people were in full accord with their leaders, for "the multitude" (Mark 15:8) requested Pilate to adhere to his custom of releasing a prisoner to them. When he gave them the choice between Christ and Barabbas, they preferred the latter; and when the governor asked what was their pleasure concerning the former, they cried, "Crucify him" (Mark 15:13). It was to "content the people" that Pilate released Barabbas (v. 15). When Pilate reasoned with them "all the people said, his blood be on us and on our children" (Matthew 27:25). And Pilate, the administrator of the Roman law, which boasted of justice, acceded to their unjust demands.

Second, the scene. It was the outskirts of Jerusalem, a city more memorable than either Rome, London, or New York; the residence of David, the royal city, the seat of Israel's kings. The city witnessed the magnificence of Solomon's reign, and here the temple stood. Here the Lord Jesus had taught and wrought miracles, and into this city He had ridden a few days earlier seated upon an ass as the multitudes cried, "Hosanna to the son of David: Blessed is he that cometh in the name of the Lord; Hosanna in the highest" (Matthew 21:9)—so fickle is human nature. Israel had rejected their King and therefore He was conducted beyond the bounds of the city, so that He "suffered without the gate" (Heb. 13:12). The actual place of the crucifixion was Golgotha, signifying "the place of a skull." Nature had anticipated the awful deed, since the contour of the ground resembled a death's head. Luke gives the Gentile name "Calvary" (Luke 23:33), for the guilt of that death rested on both Jew and Gentile.

Third, the time. This was as significant and suggestive as the historical and topographical associations of the place itself. Christ was crucified on the fourteenth of Nisan, or about the beginning of April. It was the first of Israel's great national feasts, the most important season in the Jewish year. It was the Passover, a solemn celebration of that night when all the firstborn sons of the Hebrews were spared from the angel of death in the land of Egypt. At this season great multitudes thronged Jerusalem, for it was one of the three annual occasions when every male Israelite was commanded to appear before Jehovah in the temple (Deut. 16:16). Thus, huge crowds had journeyed there from all parts of the land. It was in no obscure corner nor in secret that the Great Sacrifice was offered up to God. And the fourteenth of Nisan was the day appointed for it, for the Lord Jesus was the antitypical Lamb. "Christ our passover is sacrificed for us" (1 Cor. 5:7). On no other day could He be slain. At an earlier date they "sought to take him: but no man laid hands on him, because his hour was not yet come" (John 7:30).

"They crucified him . . . and sitting down they watched him there." My divisions are simple: what they saw; what I see; what do you see?

What They Saw

They behold the most amazing event of all history, the most awe-inspiring spectacle men ever saw, the most tragic and yet the most glorious deed ever performed. They beheld God incarnate taken by wicked hands and slain— and at the same time the Redeemer voluntarily laying down His life for those who have forfeited every claim upon Him. To the soldiers it was an ordinary event, the execution of a criminal; and thus it is with most who hear the

Gospel. It falls on their ears as a religious commonplace. To the Roman soldiers, at least for a while, Christ appeared only as a dying Jew; thus it is with the multitude today.

They beheld the incomparable perfections of the Crucified One. How immeasurably different the mien of the suffering Savior from what they had witnessed from others in similar circumstances! No cursing of His lot, no reviling of His enemies, no maledictions upon themselves. The very reverse. His lips are engaged in prayer. "Father", He says, "forgive them; for they know not what they do" (Luke 23:34). How amazed they must have been as they heard the Blessed One on the tree making "intercession for the transgressors" (Isa. 53:12). The two thieves crucified with Him mocked the Redeemer (Matthew 27:44); but at the eleventh hour one of them was "granted repentance unto life" (Acts 11:18). Turning to Jesus, he said, "Lord, remember me when thou comest into thy kingdom" (Luke 23:42). The Lord did not decline his appeal and say, "you have sinned beyond the reach of mercy"; but answered, 'Verily, I say unto thee, To day shalt thou be with me in paradise" (v. 43). They witnessed an unparalleled display of sovereign grace to one of the greatest of sinners.

They beheld most mysterious phenomena. They sat down to "watch Him," but after a while they were no longer able to do so. At midday it suddenly became midnight. "From the sixth hour [after sunrise] there was darkness over all the land unto the ninth hour" (Matthew 27:45). It was as though the sun refused to shine on such a scene, as though nature itself mourned over such a sight. During those three hours a transaction took place between Christ and God which was infinitely too sacred for finite eyes to gaze upon, a mystery which no mortal mind can fully enter. As soon as the Savior committed His spirit into the hands of the Father, "Behold, the veil of the temple was rent in twain from the top to the bottom, and the earth did quake and the rocks rent; and the graves were opened; and many bodies of the saints which slept arose" (Matthew 27:51-52). This was no ordinary sufferer; it was the Creator of heaven and earth, and heaven and earth expressed their sympathy.

They beheld and heard what was blessed to their conviction and conversion. Pharaoh witnessed a most remarkable display of God's power in the plagues which He sent upon Egypt, but far from inclining him to repentance he continued to harden his heart. Thus it always is with the unregenerate while they are left to themselves; neither the most astonishing tokens of God's goodness nor the most awe-inspiring of judgments melt them. But God was pleased to soften the callous hearts of these Roman soldiers and illumine their heathen minds. "Now when the centurion, and they that were with him, watching Jesus, saw the earthquake, and those things that were done, they feared greatly, saying, Truly this was the Son of God" (Matthew 27:54).

We regard this as another of the miracles at Calvary—a miracle of amazing grace. And we expect to meet in heaven the man who hammered the nails into the Savior's hands and thrust the spear into His side—God's answer to Christ's prayer, "Father, forgive them." So there is hope for the vilest sinner if he will surrender to the Lordship of Christ and trust in His blood.

What I See

I see an unveiling of the character of man. "Now all things that are discovered [margin] are made manifest by the light: for whatsoever doth make manifest is light" (Eph. 5:13). Christ is "the true light" (John 1:9)—the essential, divine, all-revealing light; consequently all men and all things stood exposed in His presence. The worst things predicated in Scripture of fallen human nature were exemplified in the days of Christ. God says that the heart of man is "desperately wicked" (Jer. 17:9), and it was so demonstrated by the treatment of His beloved Son. Scarcely was He born into this world than men made a determined effort to slay Him. Though He constantly went about doing good, relieving the distressed, and ministering to the souls and bodies of the needy, He was so little appreciated that He had to say, "The foxes have holes and the birds of the air have nests, but the Son of man hath not where to lay his head" (Matthew 8:20). On one occasion "they besought him that he would depart out of their coasts" (Matthew 8:34).

Not only was Christ unwelcome here, but also men hated Him "without a cause" (John 15:25). He gave them every reason to admire Him, but they had an inveterate aversion for Him. The Word declares, "the carnal mind is enmity against God" (Rom. 8:7). Multitudes go through the form of paying homage to God, but of a "god" of their own imagination. They hate the living God, and were it possible would rid the universe of Him. This is clear from their treatment of Christ, for He was none other than "God manifest in flesh" (1 Tim. 3:16). They hated and hounded Him to death, and nothing short of death by crucifixion would appease them. At Calvary the real character of man was revealed, and the desperate wickedness of his heart laid bare.

I see an unveiling of sin. Sin! That "abominable thing," which the Lord hates (Jer. 44:4), is regarded so lightly by those who commit it. Sin! It caused our first parents to be banished from Eden and is responsible for all the woe in the world. Sin! It produces strife and bloodshed and has turned this "land of the living" into a mammoth cemetery. Sin! A hideous monster we so much dislike hearing about and which we are so ready to excuse. Sin ! Satan employs all his subtle arts to render it attractive, and sets it forth in the most appealing colors. One of the great designs of the incarnation was to bring to light the hidden things of darkness. The presence here of the Holy One served as a brilliant light in a long-neglected room, revealing its squalor and filth. "If I had not come and spoken unto them, they had not had sin: but now they have no cloke for their sin" (John 15:22).

Christ here spoke comparatively. Evil as man had shown himself through history, the coming of Immanuel to earth brought sin to a head. All that had gone before was a trifling thing when compared to the monstrous wickedness done against Love incarnate. In the treatment the Son of God received at the hands of men we see sin in its true colors, stripped of all disguise, exposed in all its hideous reality, in its true nature as rebellion against God. At Calvary we behold the climax of sin, the fearful, horrible lengths to which it is capable of going. What germinated in Eden culminated in the crucifixion. The first sin occasioned spiritual suicide, the second fratricide (Cain murdered his brother): but here at Calvary it resulted in Deicide, the slaying of the Lord of glory. We also see the fearful wages of sin—death and separation from God. Since Christ hung there as the Sinbearer, He received the punishment due to them.

I see an unveiling of the character of God. The heavens declare His glory and the firmament shows His handiwork, but nowhere are His perfections more prominently displayed than at the cross. Here is His ineffable holiness. The holiness of God is the delight He has in all that is pure and lovely; therefore His nature burns against whatever is evil. God hates sin wherever it is found and He made no exception of Christ when He saw it imputed on His beloved Son. There God "laid on him the iniquity of us all" (Isa. 53:6). He dealt with Him accordingly, pouring out His holy wrath upon Him. God is "of purer eyes than to behold evil, and canst not look on iniquity" (Hab. 1:13); therefore He turned His back on the Sinbearer. "My God, my God, why hast thou forsaken me?" the suffering Savior cried, then answered His own query, "Thou art holy" (Ps. 22:1, 3).

I see God's inflexible justice. The pronouncement of His Law is, "the soul that sinneth it shall die." No deviation from it can be made, for Jehovah has expressly declared He "will by no means clear the guilty" (Ex. 34:7). But will He not make an exception of the One whom He testifies is the Lamb "without blemish and without spot" (1 Pet. 1:19)? No! For though Christ was sinless both by nature and action, because the sins of His people had been laid upon Him, God "spared not his own Son" (Rom. 8:32). Because sin was transferred to Him, punishment must be visited upon Him. Therefore, God cried, "Awake O sword, against my shepherd, and against the man that is my fellow, saith the LORD of hosts: smite the shepherd" (Zech. 13:7). God would not abate one iota of His righteous demand or allow sentiment to sully the fair face of His government. He claims to be par excellence the Judge who is "without respect of persons." How fully that was demonstrated at Calvary by His refusal to exempt the person of His Beloved, the One in whom His soul delighted (Isa. 42:1), when He occupied the place of the guilty.

I see God's amazing grace. "God commendeth his love toward us [His people], in that, while we were yet sinners, Christ died for us" (Rom. 5:8). Had He so pleased, God could have consigned the whole of Adam's race to everlasting woe. That is what each of us richly deserves. And why should He not do so? By nature we are depraved and corrupt; by practice incorrigible rebels, with no love for Him nor concern for His glory. But out of His own goodness He determined to save a people from their sins, to redeem them by Christ "to the praise of the glory of his grace" (Eph. 1:6). He determined to pluck them as brands from the burning so they might be the eternal monuments of His mercy. Because it was wholly outside their power to make atonement for their fearful crimes, He Himself provided an all-sufficient sacrifice for them. He is "the God of all grace" (1 Pet. 5:10) and He has given innumerable tokens of this. But nowhere were the "riches of His grace" so lavishly and wondrously displayed as at Calvary.

See here God's manifold wisdom. The Word declares, "There shall in no wise enter into it any thing that defileth, neither whatsoever worketh abomination" (Rev. 21:27); then how is it possible that I can ever gain admittance into the heavenly Jerusalem? How can it be that one so completely devoid of righteousness could ever receive divine approbation? The Law says, "The soul that sinneth it shall die." I have sinned and broken the Law, how then can I escape its penalty? Since I am a spiritual pauper how can the necessary ransom be procured? These are problems that no human intelligence can solve. Nor is the knot to be cut by an appeal to the bare mercy of God, for His mercy is not an attribute which overrides His justice and integrity. But at the Cross the divine perfections shone out in glorious unity like the blending of the colors in the rainbow. There "Mercy and truth met together; righteousness and peace have kissed each other" (Ps. 85:10). God's justice was satisfied by Christ and therefore His mercy flows freely to all who repent and believe. The wisdom of God appears in creation and providence, but nowhere so grandly as at the cross.

I see myself. What? Yes, as I turn my gaze to the cross I behold myself, and so does everyone who looks with the eye of faith. Christ hung there as the Surety of His people, and there cannot be representation without identification. Christ identified with those whose sins He bears, believers identified with Him. In the sight of God they are one. Christ took my place, and faith appropriates that fact. In the person of my Substitute I satisfied every requirement of God's Law. In the person of Christ I paid the full price which divine justice demanded. In the person of Christ I stand approved before God, for I am clothed with His meritorious perfections (Isa. 61:10). The whole ransomed Church of God can say of Christ, "He was wounded for our transgressions and bruised for our iniquities" (Isa. 53:4), "Who his own self bare our sins in his own body on the tree" (1 Pet. 2:24). And faith individualizes it and declares, "I am crucified with Christ . . . who loved me, and gave himself for me" (Gal. 2:20). Hallelujah! What a Savior.

What Do You See?

You behold One whom you despise and reject, if you are unsaved. Perhaps you deny it, saying my attitude is merely negative. You err. If you are not the friend of Christ you are His enemy. There is no third class. "He that is not with me is against me" (Matthew 12:30) is His own verdict, and from that there is no appeal. You have despised His authority, flouted His laws, treated His claims with contempt. You reject His yoke and scepter and refuse to be ruled by Him; thus you unite with those who cast Him out and hounded Him to death.

You behold One who is presented as Savior. Yes, despite your wicked treatment of Him hitherto, He is set before you in the Gospel as One willing and able to heal the wounds sin has made and to save your souls from eternal death. If you will throw down the weapons of your warfare against Him, surrender to His Lordship, and trust in His redeeming blood, He will accept you now. "Him that cometh to me I will in no wise cast out" (John 6:37).

You behold the One who is to be your Judge if you refuse to accept Him as Savior. Come to Him now as a repentant sinner, as a spiritual pauper, casting yourself upon His grace, and He will pardon your iniquities and give you a royal welcome. "Come unto me, all ye that labor and are heavy laden, and I will give you rest" (Matthew 11:28) is His own invitation with promise. But continue to turn your back upon Him and one day He will say to you, "Depart from me, ye cursed into everlasting fire, prepared for the devil and his angels" (Matthew 25:41).

CHAPTER 10
The Redemption of Christ

Our Righteous Redeemer—does such a title have a strange sound to the reader? Is that adjective unfamiliar in such a context? The great majority of us probably are far more accustomed to such expressions as "our loving Redeemer" and "our gracious Redeemer," or even "our mighty Redeemer." We employ the term here not because we are striving for originality. No, rather such an appellation is required by the teaching of Scripture. In fact, if we carefully observe where the Holy Spirit has placed His emphasis it is incumbent on us that we should conform our terminology thereto. See how many passages you can recall where either "loving" or "gracious" is used as an adjective in connection with Christ. If memory fails, consult a concordance, and you will be surprised that neither of them occurs a single time! Now try the word "righteous" and see how many passages refer to the Lord Jesus as such.

Christ is referred to as "my righteous servant" (Isa. 53:11); as "a righteous Branch" (Jer. 23:5); and in the next verse as "The Lord Our Righteousness"; as "the sun of righteousness" (Mal. 4:2): as a "righteous man" (Luke 23:47); as "the righteous judge" (2 Tim. 4:8). He is seen as the antitypical Melchizedek or "King of righteousness" (Heb. 7:2-3); as our "advocate with the Father," "Jesus Christ the righteous" (1 John 2:1). In addition, the same Greek word "dikaios" is rendered "just" in the following passages: Pilate's wife sent a warning to her husband, "Have thou nothing to do with this just [righteous] man" (Matthew 27:19); in the same chapter Pilate himself declared, "I am innocent of the blood of this just person" (v. 34). He is called "the just" (Acts 3:14; James 5:6); and "the just one" (Acts 7:52; 22:14); while in 1 Peter 3:18 are the well-known words, "Christ also hath once suffered for sins, the just for the unjust"—actually rendered "the righteous for the unrighteous" (ARV). When Zechariah predicted His entry into Jerusalem, riding on an ass, he said, "Behold, thy king cometh to thee, he is just"; in Revelation 19:11, where He is depicted on a white horse, it is said, "in righteousness he doth judge and make war."

In all of these passages, the Father's "fellow" and equal is viewed in His official character, as the God-man Mediator. Equally evident is that the verses intimate the Lord Jesus is righteous in His person, in the administration of His office, in the discharge of the Great Commission given Him. Before His incarnation it was announced "righteousness shall be the girdle of his loins, and faithfulness the girdle of his reins" (Isa. 11:5); and Christ affirmed by the spirit of prophecy, "I have preached righteousness in the great congregation" (Ps. 40:9). There was no fault or failure in His performing of the honoured and momentous task committed to Him, as His own words to the Father prove: "I have glorified thee on the earth. I have finished the work which thou gavest me to do" (John 17:4). God's owning of Christ as "my righteous servant" signifies that He excellently executed the work entrusted to Him. As the Holy Spirit declares, He "was faithful to him that appointed him" (Heb. 3:2). When the Father rewarded Him He said, "Thou lovest righteousness, and hatest wickedness" (Ps. 45:7).

Further, Christ is the righteous Redeemer of His people because their righteousness is in Him. He wrought out a perfect righteousness for them. Upon their believing in Him, it is imputed or reckoned to their account; therefore He is designated "The Lord Our Righteousness" (Jer. 23:6). Christ was righteous not as a private person, not for Himself alone, but for us sinners and our salvation. He acted as God's righteous Servant and as His people's righteous sponsor. He lived and died that all the infinite merits of His obedience might be made over to them. In justifying His sinful people God neither disregarded nor dishonored His law; instead He "established" it (Rom. 3:31). The Redeemer was "made under the law" (Gal. 4:4). Its strictness was not relaxed nor was one iota of its requirements abated in connection with Him. Christ rendered to the Law a personal, perfect, and perpetual obedience: therefore He did "magnify the law, and make it honorable" (Isa. 42:21). Consequently God is not only gracious but "just" at the very moment He is "the justifier of him which believeth in Jesus" (Rom. 3:26), because Jesus satisfied every requirement of righteousness on behalf of all who trust in Him.

In the righteous Redeemer we find the answer to the question, "How can those who have no righteousness of their own and who are utterly unable to procure any, become righteous before God?" How can man, who is a mass of corruption, draw nigh unto the ineffably Holy One, and look up into His face in peace? He can do so by coming to God as unrighteous, acknowledging his inability to remove unrighteousness, and offering nothing to palliate Him. Because we were unable to reach up to the holy requirements or righteousness of the Law, God brought His righteousness down to us: "I bring near my righteousness" (Isa. 46:13). That righteousness was brought near to sinners when the Word became flesh and tabernacled among men; it is brought near to us in the Gospel, "for therein is the righteousness of God revealed from faith to faith' (Rom. 1:17). This righteousness God imputes to all who believe and then deals with them according to its deserts.

"For he [God] hath made him [Christ] to be sin for us, who knew no sin; that we might be [not put into a capacity of acquiring a righteousness of our own, but] made the righteousness of God in him" (2 Cor. 5:21). Here is the double imputation of our sins to Christ and of His righteousness to us. We are not said to be made righteous, but "righteousness" itself; and not righteousness only, but "the righteousness of God" the utmost that language can reach. In the same manner that Christ was "made sin," we are made "righteousness.'' Christ did not know actual sin, but in His mediatorial interposition on our behalf He was dealt with as a guilty person. Likewise we are destitute of all legal righteousness; yet upon receiving Christ, we are viewed by the divine majesty as righteous creatures. Both were by imputation; an amazing exchange! So as to exclude the idea that any inherent righteousness is involved, it is said, "we are made the righteousness of God in Him." As the sin imputed to Christ is inherent in us, so the righteousness by which we are justified is inherent in Him.

The divine plan of redemption fully satisfies the claims of the Law. There was nothing in all its sacred injunctions which Christ did not perform, nothing in its awful threatenings which He did not sustain. He fulfilled all its precepts by an unspotted purity of heart and a perfect integrity of life. He exhausted the whole curse when He hung on the cross, abandoned by God, for the sins of His people. His obedience conferred higher honor upon the Law than it could possibly have received from an uninterrupted compliance by Adam and his posterity. The perfections of God, which were dishonored by our rebellion, are glorified in our redemption. In redemption God appears inflexibly just in exacting vengeance, and inconceivably rich in showing mercy. "The sword of justice and the scepter of grace has each its due exercise, each its full expression" (James Hervey). The interests of holiness are also secured, for where redemption is received by faith it kindles in the heart an intense hatred of sin and the deepest love and gratitude to God.

CHAPTER 11
The Saviorhood of Christ

"My thoughts are not your thoughts, neither are your ways my ways, Saith the LORD" (Isa. 55:8). Solemnly these words manifest the terrible havoc sin has wrought in fallen mankind. They are out of touch with their Maker; nay more, they are "alienated from the life of God through the ignorance that is in them, because of the blindness of their heart" (Eph. 4:18). As a consequence, the soul has lost its anchorage, everything has been thrown out of gear, and human depravity has turned all things upside down. Instead of subordinating the concerns of this life to the interests of the life to come, man devotes himself principally to the present and gives little or no thought to the eternal. Instead of putting the good of his soul ahead of the needs of the body, man is occupied chiefly about food and raiment. Instead of man's great aim being to please God, ministering to self has become his prime business.

Man's thoughts ought to be governed by God's Word, and his ways regulated by God's revealed will. But the converse is true. So the things which are of great price in the sight of God (1 Pet. 3:4) are despised by the fallen creature, and "that which is highly esteemed among men is abomination in the sight of God" (Luke 16:15). Man has turned things topsy turvy, sadly in evidence when he attempts to handle divine matters. The perversity which sin has caused appears in our reversing God's order. The Scripture speaks of man's "spirit and soul and body" (1 Thess. 5:23), but when the world refers to it, it says "body, soul, and spirit." Scripture declares that Christians are "strangers and pilgrims" in this scene; but nine times out of ten, even good men talk and write of "pilgrims and strangers."

This tendency to reverse God's order is part of fallen man's nature. Unless the Holy Spirit interposes and works a miracle of grace, its effects are fatal to the soul. Nowhere do we have a more tragic example of this than in the evangelistic message now being given, though scarcely anyone seems aware of it. That something is radically wrong with the world is widely recognized.

That Christendom is in a sad state many are painfully conscious—that error abounds on every side, that practical godliness is at a low ebb, that worldliness has devitalized many churches, is apparent to increasing numbers. But few see how bad things are, few perceive that things are rotten to the very foundation; yet such is the case.

God's true way of salvation is little known today. The Gospel which is being preached, even in orthodox circles, is often an erroneous gospel. Even there man has reversed God's order. For many years it has been taught that nothing more is required for a sinner's salvation than to "accept Christ as his personal Savior." Later, he ought to bow to Him as Lord, consecrate his life to Him, and serve Him fully. But even if he fails to do so, heaven is sure for him. He will lack peace and joy now, and probably miss some millennial crown; but having received Christ as his personal Savior, he has been delivered from wrath to come. This is a reversal of God's order. It is the devil's lie, and only the day to come will show how many have been fatally deceived by it.

We are aware this is strong language, and it may come as a shock; but test it by this light: Every passage of the New Testament where these two titles occur together say "Lord and Savior," and never "Savior" (Luke 1:46-47). Unless Jehovah had first become her "Lord," most certainly He would not have been her "Savior." No one who seriously ponders the matter has any difficulty perceiving this. How could a thrice-holy God save one who scorned His authority, despised His honor, and flouted His revealed will. It is infinite grace that God is ready to be reconciled to us when we throw the weapons of our rebellion against Him; but it would be an act of unrighteousness, putting a premium upon lawlessness, were He to pardon the sinner before he was first reconciled to His Maker.

The saints of God are bidden to make their "calling and election sure" (2 Pet. 1:10) (and this, by adding to their faith the other graces enumerated in vv. 5-7). They are assured that if they do so they shall never fall, for so an entrance shall be ministered to them abundantly "into the everlasting kingdom of our [1] Lord and [2] Savior Jesus Christ" (2 Pet. 1:11). But particularly note the order in which Christ's titles are mentioned: it is not "our Savior and Lord," but "Lord and Savior." He becomes the Savior of none until the heart and will unreservedly receive Him as Lord.

"For if after they have escaped the pollutions of the world through the knowledge of the Lord and Savior Jesus Christ, they are again entangled therein, and overcome, the latter end is worse with them than the beginning" (2 Pet. 2:20). Here the apostle refers to those who had a head knowledge of the Truth, and then apostatized. There had been a reformation outwardly in their lives, but no regeneration of the heart. For a while they were delivered from the pollution of the world, but with no supernatural work of grace having been wrought in their souls, the lustings of the flesh proved too strong. They were again overcome and returned to their former manner of life like the "dog to its vomit" or the "sow to its wallowing in the mire." The apostasy is described as, "to turn from the holy commandment delivered unto them," which referred to the terms of discipleship made known in the Gospel. But what we are particularly concerned about is the Holy Spirit's order: these apostates had been favored with the "knowledge of (1) the Lord and (2) Savior Jesus Christ."

God's people are exhorted to "grow in grace, and in the knowledge of our Lord and Savior Jesus Christ" (2 Pet. 3:18). Here again God's order is the opposite of man's. Nor is this merely a technical detail, concerning which a mistake is of little moment. No, the subject is basic, vital and fundamental, and error at this point is fatal. Those who have not submitted to Christ as Lord, but who trust in Him as Savior are deceived.

The same principle is illustrated in passages where other titles of Christ occur. Take the opening verse of the New Testament (Matthew 1:1) where He is presented as "Jesus Christ, [1] the son of David, [2] the son of Abraham." Waiving the dispensational signification of these titles, view them from the doctrinal and practical viewpoint, which should be our first consideration. "Son of David" brings in the throne, emphasizes His authority, and demands allegiance to His scepter. And "son of David" comes before "son of Abraham!" Again, we are told that God had exalted Jesus to his own right hand "to be [1] a Prince and [2] a Savior" (Acts 5:31). The concept embodied in the title "Prince" is that of supreme dominion and authority, "The prince of the kings of the earth" (Rev. 1:5).

In the Book of Acts we quickly discover that the message of the apostles was altogether different—not only in emphasis, but also in substance—from the preaching of our times. On the day of Pentecost Peter declared, "Whosoever shall call on the name of the Lord shall be saved" (Acts 2:21), and reminded his hearers that God had made Jesus "both Lord and Christ" (Acts 2:36), not Christ and Lord. To Cornelius and his household Peter presented Christ as "Lord of all" (Acts 10:36). When Barnabas came to

Antioch, he "exhorted them all, that with purpose of heart they should cleave unto the Lord" (Acts 11:23); also Paul and Barnabas "commended them to the Lord, on whom they believed" (Acts 14:23). At the great synod in Jerusalem, Peter reminded his fellows that the Gentiles would "seek after [not only a Savior, but] the Lord" (Acts 15:17). To the Philippian jailor and his household Paul and Silas preached "the word of the Lord" (Acts 16:32).

The apostles not only emphasized the Lordship of Christ, but also they made surrender to it essential to salvation. This is clear from many other passages: "And believers were the more added to [not Christ, but] the Lord" (Acts 5:14); "And all that dwelt at Lydda and Saron saw him, and turned to the Lord" (Acts 9:35); "And many believed in the Lord" (Acts 9:42); "And much people was added unto the Lord" (Acts 11:24). "Then the deputy, when he saw what was done, believed, being astonished at the doctrine of the Lord" (Acts 13:12); "And Crispus, the chief ruler of the synagogue, believed on the Lord with all his house" (Acts 18:8).

Few today have a right conception of what a scriptural and saving conversion is. The call to it is set forth in Isaiah 55:7, "Let the wicked forsake his way, and the unrighteous man his thoughts: and let him return [having in Adam departed] unto the LORD, and He will have mercy upon him." The character of conversion is described in 1 Thessalonians 1:9, "Ye turned to God from idols to serve the living and true God." Conversion, then, is a turning from sin unto holiness, from self unto God, from Satan unto Christ. It is the voluntary surrender of ourselves to the Lord Jesus, not only by a consent of dependence upon His merits, but also by a willing readiness to obey Him, giving up the keys of our hearts and laying them at His feet. It is the soul declaring, "O LORD our God, other lords beside thee have had dominion over us [namely, the world, the flesh, and the devil]: but by thee only will we make mention of thy name" (Isa. 26:13).

Conversion consists in our being recovered from our present sinfulness to the moral image of God, or, which is the same thing, to a real conformity to the moral law. But a conformity to the moral law consists in a disposition to love God supremely, live to Him ultimately, and delight in Him superlatively, and to love our neighbor as ourselves: and a practice agreeing thereto. And therefore conversion consists in our being recovered from what we are by nature to such a disposition and practice (James Bellamy, 1770).

Note the searching words in Acts 3:26, "Unto you first God having raised up his Son Jesus, sent him to bless you in turning away every one of you from his iniquities." This is Christ's way of blessing men—converting them. However the Gospel may instruct and enlighten men, so long as they remain the slaves of sin, it has conferred upon them no eternal advantage. "Know ye not that to whom ye yield yourselves servants to obey, his servants ye are to whom ye obey; whether of sin unto death, or of obedience unto righteousness?" (Rom. 6:16).

There is a very real difference between believing in the deity of Christ and surrendering to His lordship. Many are firmly persuaded that Jesus is the Son of God; they have no doubt He is the Maker of heaven and earth. But that is no proof of conversion. The demons owned Him as the "Son of God" (Matthew 8:29). What we press here is not the mind's assent to the Godhood of Christ, but the will's yielding to His authority, so that the life is regulated by His commandments. There must be a subjecting of ourselves to Him. The one is useless without the other. "He became the author of eternal salvation unto all them that obey him" (Heb. 5:9).

Yet in the face of the clear teaching of Holy Writ, when unsaved people are concerned about their future destiny, and inquire, "What must we do to be saved?" the answer they are usually given is, "Accept Christ as your personal Savior." Little effort is made to press upon them (as Paul did the Philippian jailor) the Lordship of Christ. Many a blind leader of the blind glibly quotes, "But as many as received him, to them gave He power to become the sons of God" (John 1:12). Perhaps the leader objects, "But nothing is said there about receiving Christ as Lord." Directly, no; nor is anything said there about receiving Christ "as a personal Savior"! It is a whole Christ which must be received, or none at all.

But if the objector will carefully ponder the context of John 1:12, he will quickly discover that it is as Lord Christ is presented, and as such must be received by us. In the previous verse, "He came unto his own, and his own received him not." In what character does that view Him? Clearly, as the Owner and Master of Israel; and it was as such they "received him not." Consider what He does for those who do receive Him: "to them gave he power [the right or prerogative] to become the sons of God." Who but the Lord of lords is vested with authority to give others the title to be sons of God!

In an unregenerate state, no sinner is subject to Christ as Lord, though he may be fully convinced of His deity, and employ "Lord Jesus" when referring to Him. When we say that no unregenerate person "is subject to

Christ as Lord," we mean that His will is not the rule of life; to please, obey, honor, and glorify Christ is not the dominant aim, disposition, and striving of the heart. Far from this being the case, his real sentiment is, "Who is the LORD, that I should obey His voice?" (Ex. 5:2). The whole trend of his life is saying, "I will not have this man to reign over me" (see Luke 19:14). Despite all religious pretensions, the real attitude of the unregenerate toward God is, "Depart from us; for we desire not the knowledge of thy ways. What is the Almighty, that we should serve [be in subjection to] him?" (Job 21:14-15). Their conduct intimates, "our lips are our own: who is lord over us?" (Ps. 12:4). Instead of surrendering to God in Christ, every sinner turns "to his own way" (Isa. 53:6), living only to please self.

When the Holy Spirit convicts of sin, He causes that person to see what sin really is. He makes the convicted one understand that sin is rebellion against God, a refusal to submit to the Lord. The Spirit causes him to realize that he has been an insurrectionist against Him who is exalted above all. He is now convicted not only of this sin, or that idol, but also is brought to realize his whole life has been a fighting against God; that he has knowingly, willfully, and constantly ignored and defied Him, deliberately choosing to go his own way. The work of the Spirit in God's elect is not so much to convince each of them they are lost sinners (the conscience of the natural man knows that, without any supernatural operation of the Spirit!); it is to reveal the exceeding "sinfulness of sin" (Rom. 7:13), by making us see and feel that all sin is a species of spiritual anarchy, a defiance of the Lordship of God.

When a man has really been convicted by the supernatural operation of the Holy Spirit, the first effect on him is complete and abject despair. His case appears to be utterly hopeless. He now sees he has sinned so grievously that it appears impossible for a righteous God to do anything but damn him for eternity. He sees what a fool he has been in heeding the voice of temptation, fighting against the Most High, and in losing his own soul. He recalls how often God has spoken to him in the past—as a child, as a youth, as an adult, upon a bed of sickness, in the death of a loved one, in adversities—and how he refused to listen and deliberately turned a deaf ear. He now feels he has sinned away his day of grace.

But the ground must be plowed and harrowed before it is receptive to seed. So the heart must be prepared by these harrowing experiences, the stubborn will broken, before it is ready for the healing of the Gospel. But how very few ever are savingly convicted by the Spirit! The Spirit continues His work in the soul, plowing still deeper, revealing the hideousness of sin, producing a horror of and hatred for it. The sinner next receives the beginning of hope, which results in an earnest inquiry, "What must I do to be saved?" Then the Spirit, who has come to earth to glorify Christ, presses upon that awakened soul the claims of His Lordship (i.e. Luke 14:26-33) and makes us realize that Christ demands our hearts, lives, and all. Then He grants grace to the quickened soul to renounce all other lords, to turn away from all idols and to receive Christ as Prophet, Priest, and King.

Nothing but the sovereign and supernatural work of the Spirit can bring this to pass. A preacher may induce a man to believe what Scripture says about his lost condition, persuade him to bow to the divine verdict, and then accept Christ as his personal Savior. No man wants to go to hell, and fire is assured intellectually that Christ stands ready as a fire escape, on the sole condition that he jump into His arms ("rest on His finished work"), thousands will do so. But a hundred preachers are unable to make an unregenerate person realize the dreadful nature of sin, or show him that he has been a lifelong rebel against God, or change his heart so that he now hates himself and longs to please God and serve Christ. Only the Spirit can bring man to the place where he is willing to forsake every idol, cut off a hindering right hand or pluck out an offending right eye.

Probably some will say, "But the exhortations addressed to saints in the epistles show that it is Christians, and not the unsaved, who are to surrender to Christ's Lordship (Rom. 12:1). Such a mistake only serves to demonstrate the gross spiritual darkness which has enveloped even orthodox Christendom. The exhortations of the epistles simply signify that Christians are to continue as they began, "As ye have therefore received Christ Jesus the Lord, so walk ye in him" (Col. 2:6). All the exhortations may be summed up in two words: "Come to Christ," "Abide in Him"; and what is abiding but coming to Christ constantly (1 Pet. 2:4)? The saints (Rom. 12:1) had already been bidden to "yield" themselves "unto God" (Rom. 6:13). While we are on earth we will always need such admonitions. The backslidden church at Ephesus was told, "Repent, and do the first works" (Rev. 2:5).

And now a pointed question: Is Christ your Lord? Does He in fact occupy the throne of your heart? Does He actually rule your life? If not, then most certainly He is not your Savior. Unless your heart has been renewed, unless grace has changed you from a lawless rebel to a loving subject, then you are yet in your sins, on the broad road to destruction.

CHAPTER 12
The Lordship of Christ

"But sanctify in your hearts Christ as Lord" (1 Pet. 3:15, RV). In view of the context it is striking to note that it was Peter whom the Spirit of God first moved to write these words. As he did so, his heart, no doubt, was filled with sorrow and deep contrition. He says, "If ye suffer for righteousness' sake, happy are ye: and be not afraid of their terror, neither be troubled" (v. 14). On a never-to-be forgotten occasion, he had been afraid of the "terror" of the wicked. In Pilate's palace the fear of man brought him a snare. But in our text he announces the divine remedy for deliverance from the fear of man.

"But sanctify in your hearts Christ as Lord." In the light of its setting, this means, first of all, to let the awe of the lordship of Christ possess your hearts. Dwell constantly on the fact that Christ is Lord. Because He is Lord, all power in heaven and earth is His; therefore He is Master of every situation, sufficient for every emergency, able to supply every need. When a Christian trembles in the presence of his enemies, it is because he doubts or has lost sight of the faithfulness and power of Christ.

"But sanctify in your hearts Christ as Lord." The motive for obeying this precept should not be our own peace and comfort, but His honor and glory. To guard against the feat of man, the saint is to cultivate the fear of the Lord, that Christ may be magnified. The Lord Jesus is glorified when His persecuted people preserve a calm demeanor and immovable fortitude in the face of all opposition. But this is possible only as our hearts are occupied with Him, and particularly with His lordship.

"But sanctify in your hearts, Christ as Lord." These words have a wider application. How little professing Christians dwell on the lordship of Christ! How sadly inadequate are the real Christian's views of that One who has a name which is above every name! "That I may know [obtain a better knowledge of] him" (Phil. 3:10), should be the daily longing of our hearts, and the earnest prayer of our lips. Not only do we need to grow in "grace" but also in "the knowledge of our Lord and Savior Jesus Christ" (2 Pet.

3:18).

How little we really know the Christ of God. "No man knoweth [perfectly] the Son, but the Father" (Matthew 11:27); yet much has been revealed concerning Him in the Scriptures. How little we study those Scriptures with the definite object of seeking a better, deeper, fuller knowledge of the Lord Jesus! How circumscribed is the scope of our studies! Many form their conceptions of Christ from the first four books of the New Testament and rarely read beyond those books.

The gospels treat of Christ's life during the days of His humiliation. They view Him in the form of a Servant, who came not to be ministered unto, but to minister. True, Matthew's Gospel sets forth the kingship of Him who was here as Jehovah's Servant; yet it is as the rejected King. True also, John's Gospel portrays the divine glories of the incarnate Son; yet as the One who was unknown in the world which He had made, and as rejected by His own to whom He came (John 1:10-11). It is not until we pass beyond the gospels that we find the lordship of Jesus of Nazareth really made manifest.

On the day of Pentecost, Peter said, "Let all the house of Israel know assuredly, that God hath made that same Jesus, whom ye have crucified, both Lord and Christ" (Acts 2:36). The humbled One is now victorious. He who was born in lowliness has been exalted "far above all principality, and power, and might, and dominion, and every name that is named, not only in this world, but also in that which is to come" (Eph. 1:21). He who suffered His face to be covered with the vile spit of men has been given a name more excellent than the angels (Heb. 1:4). He whom man crowned with thorns has been "crowned with glory and honor" (Heb. 2:9). He who hung, in apparent helplessness upon a cross has taken His seat "on the right hand of the Majesty on high" (Heb. 1:3).

The epistles, in contrast to the gospels, were all written from the viewpoint of an ascended Christ. They treat of a glorified Savior. How much we lose by their neglect! Why is it that when Christ comes to our minds our thoughts turn back to the "days of His flesh"? Why are our hearts so little occupied with the heavenly Christ? Why do we meditate so little upon His exaltation, His seat and session at God's right hand? Is it not because we read the epistles so infrequently?

Many Christians find the epistles so much more difficult than the gospels. Of course they do, because they are so unfamiliar. Enter a strange city and its layout, streets and suburbs are unknown. It is hard to find your way about.

So it is with the epistles. The Christian must live in them to become acquainted with their contents.

It is in the epistles alone that the distinctive character of Christianity is set forth; not in the gospels; the Acts is transitionary; and most of the Revelation belongs to the future. The epistles alone treat of the present dispensation. But present-day preaching rarely notices them. Christians, in their private reading of the Word, seldom turn to them. But in the Epistles only is Christianity expounded—Christianity has to do with a risen, glorified, and enthroned Christ. Thus, if we are to "Sanctify in your hearts Christ Jesus as Lord," we must spend much time in the epistles.

CHAPTER 13
The Friendship of Christ

How many have ever heard a sermon or read an article on this subject? How many of God's people think of Christ in this blessed relationship? Christ is the best Friend the Christian has, and it is both his privilege and duty to regard Him as such. Our scriptural support is in the following passages: "There is a friend that sticketh closer than a brother" (Prov. 18:24), which can refer to none other than the Lord Jesus; "This is my beloved, and this is my friend, O daughters of Jerusalem" (Song 5:16). That is the language of His Spouse, the testimony of the Church, avowing this most intimate relationship. Add to these the witness of the New Testament when Christ was termed "a friend of publicans and sinners" (Luke 7:34).

Many and varied are the relationships in which Christ stands to a believer, and he is the loser if He is ignored in any of them. Christ is God, Lord, Head, Savior of the Church. Officially He is our Prophet, Priest, and King; personally He is our Kinsman-Redeemer, our Intercessor, our Friend. That title expresses the near union between the Lord Jesus and believers. They are as if but one soul actuated them; indeed, one and the same spirit does, for "he that is joined unto the Lord is one spirit" (1 Cor. 6:17). "Christ stands in a nearer relation than a brother to the Church: He is her Husband, her Bosom-friend" (John Gill). "We are members of his body, of his flesh, and of his bones" (Eph. 5:30). But even those relationships fall short of fully expressing the nearness, spiritual oneness, and indissoluableness of the union between Christ and His people. There should be the freest approaches to Him and the most intimate fellowship with Him. To deny Christ that is to ignore the tact He is our best Friend.

"There is a Friend that sticketh closer than a brother." That endearing title not only expresses the near relation between Him and His redeemed but also the affection which He bears them. Nothing has, does, or can, dampen, or quench its outflow. "Having loved his own which were in the world, he loved them unto the end" (John 13:1). That blessed title tells of the sympathy

He bears His people in all their sufferings, temptations, and infirmities. "In all their affliction he was afflicted . . . in his love and in his pity he redeemed them; and he bare them, and carried them all the days of old" (Isa. 63:9). What demonstrations of His friendship! That title also tells of His deep concern for our interests. He has our highest welfare at heart; accordingly He has promised, "I will not turn away from them, to do them good" (Jer. 32:40). Consider more definitely the excellencies of our best Friend:

Christ is an ancient Friend. Old friends we prize highly. The Lord Jesus was our Friend when we were His enemies! We fell in Adam, but He did not cease to love us; rather He became the last Adam to redeem us and "lay down his life for his friends" (John 15:13). He sent His servants to preach the Gospel unto us, but we despised it. Even when we were wandering in the ways of folly He determined to save us, and watched over us. In the midst of our sinning and sporting with death, He arrested us by His grace, and by His love overcame our enmity and won our hearts.

Christ is a constant Friend; One that "loveth at all times" (Prov. 17:17). He continues to be our Friend through all the vicissitudes of life—no fair-weather friend who fails us when we need Him most. He is our Friend in the day of adversity, equally as much as in the day of prosperity. Was He not so to Peter? He is "a very present help in trouble" (Ps. 46:1), and evidences it by His sustaining grace. Nor do our transgressions turn away His compassion from us; even then He acts as a friend. "If any man sin, we have an advocate with the Father, Jesus Christ the righteous" (1 John 2:1).

Christ is a faithful Friend. His grace is not shown at the expense of righteousness, nor do His mercies ignore the requirements of holiness. Christ always has in view both the glory of God and the highest good of His people. "Faithful are the wounds of a friend" (Prov. 27:6). A real friend performs his duty by pointing out my faults. In this respect, too, Christ does "show himself friendly" (Prov. 18:24). Often He says to each of us, "I have a few things against thee" (Rev. 2:14)—and rebukes us by His Word, convicts our conscience by His Spirit, and chastens us by His providence "that we might be partakers of his holiness" (Heb. 12:10).

Christ is a powerful Friend. He is willing and able to help us. Some earthly friends may have the desire to help us in the hour of need, but lack the wherewithal: not so our heavenly Friend. He has both the heart to assist and also the power. He is the Possessor of "unsearchable riches," and all that He has is at our disposal. "The glory which thou gavest me I have given them"

(John 17:22). We have a Friend at court, for Christ uses His influence with the Father on our behalf. "He ever liveth to make intercession for us" (Heb. 7:25). No situation can possibly arise which is beyond the resources of Christ.

Christ is an everlasting Friend. He does not desert us in the hour of crisis. "Though I walk through the valley of the shadow of death, I will fear no evil, for thou art with me" (Ps. 23:4). Nor does death sever us from this Friend who "sticketh closer than a brother," for we are with Him that very day in paradise. Death will have separated us from those on earth, but "absent from the body" we shall be "present with the Lord" (2 Cor. 5:8). And in the future Christ will manifest Himself as our Friend, saying "Enter thou into the joy of thy Lord."

Since Christ is such a Friend to the Christian, what follows? Friendship should be answered with friendship! Negatively, there should be no coldness, aloofness, trepidation, hesitancy on our part; but positively, a free availing ourselves of such a privilege. We should delight ourselves in Him. Since He is a faithful Friend we may safely tell Him the secrets of our hearts, for He will never betray our confidence. But His friendship also imposes definite obligations—to please Him and promote His cause, and daily seek His counsel.

CHAPTER 14
The Helpfulness of Christ

One of the Apostle's purposes in writing the epistle to the Hebrews is to strengthen the faith of those who were sorely tried and wavering—and by parity of reason all who are weak in grace. "For in that he himself hath suffered being tempted, he is able to succor them that are tempted" (Heb. 2:18). The method he followed in prosecuting that end was to set forth the transcendent excellency of Christ, with His good will to the sons of men. He exhibits at length the perfections of His person, His offices, and His work. He declares that He is the Son of God, who has been made the Heir of all things; that He is the brightness of the Father's glory and the express image of His person. Full demonstration was made of His immeasurable superiority to angels, yet so infinite was His condescension and so great His love to those given Him by the Father that He took a place lower than that occupied by celestial creatures; yet, "in all things . . . to be made like unto his brethren" (Heb. 2:17). In His offices He is revealed as the supreme Prophet, the final spokesman of Deity (Heb. 1:1-2), as a glorious king (Heb. 1:8), as "a merciful and faithful high priest" (Heb. 2:17); in His work as making "reconciliation [lit. "propitiation"] for the sins of the people" (Heb. 2:17), as ever living to make intercession for them (Heb. 7:25), as "bringing many sons unto glory" (Heb. 2:10).

So amazing was the grace of this august Being that He not only partook of the nature of those He came here to save, but also He entered fully into their circumstances, became subject to their infirmities, was tempted in all respects as they are (inward corruption excepted). He shed His precious blood and died a shameful death in their stead and on their behalf; and all of this to manifest the reality and abundance of His mercy unto sinners, fire their hearts, and draw out the affections of believers to Him. The apostle points out one of the blessed consequences of the Son's having become incarnate and entered into fellowship with His suffering people. First, the Lord of glory came down into the realm of temptation. Scripture is always to be understood in its widest possible latitude; therefore "tempt" is signifying put to the proof, subjected to trials and troubles, solicited to evil. Christ was tempted by God, by men, by the devil. Second, He "suffered" while being tempted. Those temptations were not mere make-believe, but real and painful. It could not be otherwise, for not only did He partake of all human sensibilities, but also His holiness felt acutely every form of evil. Third, the remembrance of His sufferings makes Him the more mindful of ours.

"For in that he himself hath suffered being tempted, he is able to succor them that are tempted." Let us consider first the timeliness and preciousness of those words to those to whom they were originally addressed. The Hebrews saints were Jews who had been convened in the days of Christ and under the preaching of the apostles, and they were in peculiarly trying circumstances. Their unconverted countrymen regarded them as apostates from Moses, and therefore from Jehovah Himself. They would have no fellowship with them, but instead regarded them with the utmost contempt and treated them most cruelly. This resulted in great distress and privation, so that they "endured a great fight of afflictions," were "made a gazingstock both by reproaches and afflictions," even to "the spoiling of their goods" (Heb. 10:32-34), because of their continued loyalty to Christ. Hence they were strongly tempted to abandon the Christian profession, resume their former place under Judaism, and thereby escape further trouble. Now it was to believers in such a situation that our text was addressed. The apostle reminds them that Christ Himself was severely tempted, that He was subjected to worse trials than ours; yet He endured the same and emerged a victorious Overcomer. Then he assured them that the Savior was able to sustain, comfort, and strengthen them.

There are Christians today who are in circumstances similar to those of the oppressed Hebrews. The world hates them, and does so in proportion to their fidelity and conformity to Christ. Some are treated harshly by ungodly relatives. Some suffer at the hands of graceless professors. Others experience divine chastisement or perplexing providences, or are passing through the waters of bereavement or a painful sickness. At such times Satan is particularly active, launching his fiercest attacks, tempting them in various ways. Here is relief—real, present, all-sufficient relief. Turn your heart and eye to the Savior, and consider how well qualified He is to succor you. He is clothed with our humanity, and therefore capable of being "touched with the feeling of our infirmities." The experience through which He passed fit Him to pity us. He knows all about your case, fully understands your trials and gauges the strength of your temptation. He is not an indifferent spectator, but full of compassion. He wept by the grave of Lazarus—and He is the same today as yesterday. He is faithful in responding to the appeals of His people.

"He is able to succor" no matter what form the temptation or trial takes. "Succour" is a comprehensive word: it means "to befriend," "to assist those in need," "to strengthen the weak." But the Greek term is even more striking and beautifully expressive: it signifies to hasten in response to a cry of distress, literally to "run in to the call" of another. Chrysostom interpreted it, "He gives out His hand unto them with all readiness." A blessed illustration is seen in the case of Christ stretching forth His hand to catch hold of Peter as he began to sink in the sea (Matthew 14:30-31). That was the Savior succouring one of His own. The same tender benevolence was yet more fully exemplified where we behold Him as the good Samaritan tending the wounded traveler (Luke 10:33-35). "He is able." The Greek word implies both fitness and a willingness to do a thing. Christ is alike competent and ready to undertake for His people. There is no unwillingness in Him. The straitness is always in us. "He is able to save them to the uttermost that come unto God by him" (Heb. 7:25) signifies readiness as well as ability.

During His sojourn on this earth, was He not ever ready to heal diseased bodies? And do you think that He is now unwilling to minister to distressed souls? Perish the thought. He was always at the disposal of the maimed, the blind, the palsied, yes, of the repellent leper too. He was ever prepared, uncomplainingly, to relieve suffering, though it cost Him something—"there went virtue out of him" (Luke 6:19)—and though much unbelief was expressed by those He befriended. As it was then apart of His mission to heal the sick, so it is now a part of His ministry to bind up the brokenhearted. What a Savior is ours! The almighty God, the all-tender Man. One who is infinitely above us in His original nature and present glory, yet One who became flesh and blood, lived on the same plane as we do, experienced the same troubles, and suffered as we, though far more acutely. Then how well qualified He is to supply your every need! Cast all your care upon Him, knowing that He cares for you.

Whatever your circumstances, the succouring Savior is all-sufficient and enters sympathetically into your condition. He knew what it was to be weary (John 4:6) and exhausted (Mark 4:36-38). He knew what it was to suffer hunger and thirst. Are you homeless? He had not a place to lay His head. Are you in straitened circumstances? He was cradled in a manger. Are you grief-stricken? He was the Man of sorrows. Are you misunderstood by fellow believers? So was He by His own disciples. Whatever your lot, He can enter fully into it. He experienced all the miseries of mankind, and has not forgotten them. Are you assailed by Satan? So was He. Do blasphemous thoughts at times torment your mind? The devil tempted Him idolatrously to worship him. Are you in such desperation as to think of making an end of yourself? Satan challenged Him to cast Himself down from the pinnacle of the temple. He "was in all points tempted like as we are, sin excepted."

Angels may pity, but they can have no fellow feeling. But Christ's compassion (to suffer with) moves Him to succor. In some instances He does so before the temptation comes, and in a variety of ways. He prepares for it by forewarning of the same; as with Israel being afflicted in Egypt (Gen. 15:13), and Paul (Acts 9:16)—in our case by causing His providences to presage the temptation; by fitting us for them, as Christ was anointed with the Spirit before the devil tempted Him; or by melting the heart with a sense of His goodness, which moves us to say,"How then can I do this great wickedness?" (Gen. 39:9).

He succours under temptation; in some cases by the powerful application of a precept or promise, which as a cable holds the heart fast amid the storm; by a providential interposition which prevents our executing the evil intention, or by removing the temptation itself; by giving us to prove the sufficiency of His grace (2 Cor. 1:2). He succours after temptation, by giving us a spirit of contrition (Luke 22:61-62), moving us to confess our sins. As angels ministered to Him after His conflict with Satan, so He ministers to us. Then no matter how dire your situation or acute your suffering, apply to Christ for relief and deliverance, and count upon His help. It is when the child is most ill that the mother comes and sits beside it (Isa. 66:13).

CHAPTER 15
The Call of Christ

"Come unto Me, all ye that labor and are heavy laden, and I will give you rest. Take my yoke upon you, and learn of me; for I am meek and lowly in heart: and ye shall find rest unto your souls. For my yoke is easy, and my burden is light" (Matthew 11:28-30).

Familiar as the sound of those words are to professing Christians, there is a pressing need for their careful examination. Few portions of God's Word have received such superficial treatment. That these verses call for prayerful meditation some will admit, but few realize that such a "simple passage" demands protracted study. Many take it for granted they already understand its meaning, hence they make no diligent inquiry into the significance of its terms. The mere fact a verse is so frequently quoted is no proof that we really see its import; yet, such familiarity has precluded careful examination and renders it far more likely we do not rightly grasp its truth.

There is a vast difference between being acquainted with the sound of a verse of Holy Writ and entering into the sense of it. Our age is marked by industrial loafing and mental slackness. Work is detested and how quickly a task may be disposed of, rather than how well it may be done, is the order of the day. The same dilatory spirit marks the products of both the pulpit and the printed page; hence the superficial treatment this passage commonly receives. No regard is paid to its context or no laborious attempt made to ascertain its coherence (the relation of one clause to another); no painstaking examination and exposition of its terms.

If ever a passage of Scripture were mutilated and its meaning perverted, it is this one. Only a fragment of it usually is quoted, with the part most unpalatable to the flesh omitted. A particular call is twisted into a promiscuous invitation by deliberately ignoring the qualifying terms there used by the Savior. Even when the opening clause is quoted, no attempt is made to show what is involved in "come to Christ," so the hearer is left to assume he already understands its meaning. The special offices in which the

Son of God is portrayed, namely as Lord and Master, as Prince and Prophet, are ignored, and another substituted. The conditional promise made by Christ is falsified by making it an unconditional one, as though His "rest" could be obtained without our taking His "yoke" upon us, and without our "learning" of Him.

Such charges may be resented bitterly by a large number of churchgoers who do not wish to hear anyone criticized. But if they are prepared to remain "at ease in Zion," if they are content whether they be deceived or not, if they have such confidence in men that they are willing to receive the most valuable things of all secondhand, if they refuse to examine their foundations and search their hearts, then we must "let them alone" (Matthew 15:14). But there are still some who prize their souls so highly they consider no effort too great to ascertain whether or not they possess a saving knowledge of God's truth; whether or not they truly understand the terms of God's salvation; whether or not they are building on an unshakable foundation.

Take a closer look at the passage. It opens with, "Come unto Me . . . and I will give you rest" and closes with, "and ye shall find rest unto your souls." It is not (as some have supposed) two different rests which are spoken of, but the same in both cases; namely, spiritual rest, saving rest. Nor are two different aspects of this rest portrayed; but rather one rest viewed from two distinct viewpoints. In the former, divine sovereignty is in view, "I will give"; in the latter, human responsibility is enforced, "ye shall find." In the opening clause Christ affirms that He is the Giver of rest; in what follows He specifies the terms upon which He dispenses rest; or to express it another way, the conditions which we must meet if we are to obtain that rest. The rest is freely given, yet only to those who comply with the revealed requirements of its Bestower.

"Come unto Me." Who issues this call? Christ, you reply. True, but Christ in what particular character? Did Christ speak as King, commanding His subjects; as Creator, addressing His creatures; as Physician, inviting the sick; or as Lord, instructing His servants? But do you draw a distinction in your mind between the person of Christ and the office of Christ? Do you not distinguish sharply between His office as Prophet, as Priest, and as King? Have you found such distinctions both necessary and helpful? Then why do people complain when we call attention to the varied relations which our Lord sustains, and the importance of noting which of these relations He is acting in at any time. Attention to such details often makes all the difference between a right and wrong understanding of a passage.

To answer our query in what particular character Christ issued this call, it is necessary to look at the verses preceding. Attention to context is one of the very first concerns for those who would carefully ponder any particular passage. Matthew 11 opens with John the Baptist having been cast into prison, from which he sent messengers to Christ to acquaint Him with his perplexity (vv. 2-3). Our Lord publicly vindicated His forerunner and magnified his unique office (vv. 4-15). Having praised the Baptist and his ministry, Christ went on to reprove those who had been privileged to enjoy both it and that of His own, because they did not profit from it, but had despised and rejected both. So depraved were the people of that day, they accused John of being demon-possessed and charged Christ with being a glutton and a winebibber (vv. 16-19).

One of the most solemn passages in Holy Writ (vv. 20-24) records some of the most fearful words which ever fell from the lips of the Son of God. He unbraided the cities where most of His mighty works were done because "they repented not" (v. 20). Note that Christ refused to gloss over the perversity of the people; instead, He charged them with their sins. And let Antinomians observe that, so far from the Christ of God ignoring human responsibility or excusing men's spiritual impotency, He held them strictly accountable and blamed them for their impenitency.

Wilful impenitency is the great damning sin of multitudes that enjoy the Gospel, and which (more than any other) sinners will be upbraided with to eternity. The great doctrine that both John the Baptist, Christ Himself, and the apostles preached, was repentance: the great thing designed to both in the "piping" and in the "mourning" was to prevail with people to change their minds and ways. to leave their sins and turn to God; but this they would not be brought to. He does not say, because they believed not, for some kind of faith many of them had, that Christ was a "Teacher come from God;" but because they "repented not"—their faith did not prevail to the transforming of their hearts and the reforming of their lives. Christ reproved them for their other sins that He might lead them to repentance, but when they repented not, He upbraided them with that as their refusal to be healed. He upbraided them with it, that they might upbraid themselves, and might at length see the folly of it, as that which alone makes the sad case a desperate one and the wound incurable (Matthew Henry).

The particular sin for which Christ upbraided them was that of impenitence. The special aggravation of their sin was that they had witnessed most of Christ's miraculous works, for in those cities the Lord had for some time resided and performed many of His miracles of healing. Some places enjoy the means of grace more plentifully than others. Just as certain parts of the earth receive a much heavier rainfall than others, certain countries and towns have been favored with purer Gospel preaching and more outpourings of the Spirit than others. God is sovereign in the distribution of His gifts, both natural and spiritual, and "unto whomsoever much is given, of him shall much be required" (Luke 12:48). The greater our opportunities the greater our obligations; and the stronger the inducements we have to repent the more heinous is impenitence, and the heavier reckoning will be. Christ notes His "mighty works" among us, and will yet hold us to an account of them.

"Woe unto thee, Chorazin! woe unto thee, Bethsaida!" (Matthew 11:21). Christ came into the world to dispense blessing. But if His person is despised, His authority rejected, and His mercies slighted, then He has terrible woes in reserve. But how many church attenders hear anything at all about this? Often the pulpiteer has deliberately taken the line of least resistance and sought only to please the pew, withholding what was unpalatable or unpopular. Souls are deceived if a sentimental Christ is substituted for the Scriptural Christ, if His "Beatitudes" (Matthew 5) are emphasized and His "woes" (Matthew 23) are ignored.

In still further aggravation of their sin of impenitence, our Lord affirmed that the citizens of Chorazin and Bethsaida were worse at heart than the Gentiles they despised. He asserted that if Tyre and Zidon had enjoyed such privileges as they, they would have "repented long ago in sackcloth and ashes." Some of the blessings Christendom despises would be welcome in many parts of heathendom.

We are not competent to solve every difficulty, or fully to understand the whole of this subject; it suffices that Christ knew the hearts of the impenitent Jews to be more hardened in rebellion and enmity, and less susceptible of suitable impressions from His doctrine and miracles, than those of the inhabitants of Tyre and Sidon would have been; and therefore their final condemnation would be proportionably more intolerable (Thomas Scott).

On the one hand this passage does not stand alone (see Ezekiel 3:6-7); on the other, the repentance spoken of by Christ is not necessarily one which leads to eternal salvation.

Still more solemn are the awful words of Christ (Matthew 11:23-24), where He announced the doom of highly favored Capernaum. Because of the unspeakable privileges enjoyed by its inhabitants, they had been lifted heavenwards. But because their hearts were so earthbound they scorned such blessings; therefore they would be "brought down to hell." The greater the advantages enjoyed, the more fearful the doom of those who abuse them; the higher the elevation, the more fatal a fall from it. Honorable Capernaum is then compared with dishonorable Sodom, which, because of its enormities, God had destroyed with fire and brimstone. It was in Capernaum the Lord Jesus had resided chiefly upon entry into His public ministry, and where so many of His miracles of healing were accomplished. Yet so obdurate were its inhabitants, so wed to their sins, they refused to apply to Him for the healing of their souls. Had such mighty works been done by Him in Sodom its people would have been affected and their city remain as a lasting monument of divine mercy.

"But I say unto you, that it shall be more tolerable for the land of Sodom in the day of judgment, than for thee" (v. 24). Yes, my reader, though you may hear nothing about it from the pulpit, there is a "day of judgment" awaiting the world. It is, "the day of wrath and revelation of the righteous judgment of God, who will render to every man according to his deeds"; it is the day "when God shall judge the secrets of men by Jesus Christ according to my gospel" (Rom. 2:5, 16); "For God shall bring every work into judgment, with every secret thing, whether it be good, or whether it be evil" (Eccl. 12:14); "The Lord knoweth how to deliver the godly out of temptations, and to reserve the unjust unto the day of judgment to be punished" (2 Pet. 2:9); The punishment then meted out will be in proportion to the opportunities given and rejected; the privileges vouchsafed and scorned; the light granted and quenched. Most intolerable will be the doom of those who have abused the greatest advancements heavenwards.

"At that time Jesus answered and said, I thank thee, O Father, Lord of heaven and earth, because thou hast hid these things from the wise and prudent, and hast revealed them unto babes" (Matthew 11:25). The connection between this and the preceding verses is most instructive. There the Lord Jesus intimates that the majority of His mighty works had produced no good effect upon those who saw them, that their beholders remained impenitent. So little influence had His gracious presence exerted upon Capernaum, where He spent much of His time, that its fate would be worse than Sodom's. Christ looks away from earth to heaven, and finds consolation in the sovereignty of God and the absolute security of His covenant. From upbraiding the impenitence of men, Christ turned to render thanks to the Father. On the word "answered," Matthew Henry said, "It is called an answer though no other words are found recorded but His own, because it is so comfortable a reply to the melancholy considerations preceding it, and is aptly set in the balance against them."

A word of warning is needed at this point, for we are such creatures of extremes. In earlier paragraphs we referred to those who substituted a sentimental Christ for the true Christ; yet the reader must not infer from this that we believe in a stoical Christ, hard, cold, devoid of feeling. Not so. The Christ of Scripture is perfect Man as well as God the Son, possessed of human sensibilities; yes, capable of much deeper feeling than any of us, whose faculties are blunted by sin. The Lord Jesus was not unaffected by grief when He pronounced the doom of those cities, nor did He view them with fatalistic indifference as He found comfort in the sovereignty of God. Scripture must be compared with Scripture: He who wept over Jerusalem (Luke 19:41) would not be unmoved as He foresaw the intolerable fate awaiting Capernaum. The fact that He was "the Man of sorrows" precludes any such concept.

A similar warning is needed by hyper-Calvinists with fatalistic stoicism:

It seems plain then, that those who are indifferent about the event of the Gospel, who satisfy themselves with this thought, that the elect shall be saved, and feel no concern for unawakened sinners, make a wrong inference from a true doctrine, and know not what spirit they are of. Jesus wept for those who perished in their sins. Paul had great grief and sorrow of heart for the Jews, though he gave them this character, "that they pleased not God, and were contrary to all men." It well becomes us, while we admire distinguishing grace to ourselves, to mourn over others: and inasmuch as secret things belong to the Lord, and we know not but some, of whom we have at present but little hopes, may at last be brought to the knowledge of the Truth, we should be patient and forebearing after the pattern of our heavenly Father, and endeavor by every proper and prudent means to stir them up to repentance, remembering that they cannot be more distant from God than by nature we were ourselves (John Newton).

As perfect Man and as "minister of the circumcision" (Rom. 15:8) the Lord Jesus felt acutely any lack of response to His arduous efforts. This is clear from His lament, "I have labored in vain, I have spent my strength for nought" (Isa. 49:4). But observe how He comforted Himself. "Yet surely my judgment is with the LORD, and my work [or "reward"] with my God" (Isa. 49:4). Thus, both in the language of prophecy and here in Matthew 11:25-26, the Lord Jesus sought relief from the discouragements of the Gospel by retreating into the divine sovereignty. "We may take great encouragement in looking upward to God, when round about us we see nothing but what is discouraging. It is sad to see how regardless most men are of their own happiness, but it is comfortable to think that the wise and faithful God will, however, effectually secure the interests of His own glory" (Matthew Henry).

Christ alluded here to the sovereignty of God in three details. First, by owning His Father as "Lord of heaven and earth," that is, as sole Proprietor thereof. It is well to remember, especially when it appears Satan is master of this lower sphere, that God not only "doeth according to His will in the army of heaven," but also "among the inhabitants of the earth," so that "none can stay his hand" (Dan. 4:35). Second, by affirming, "Thou hast hid these things from the wise and prudent." The things pertaining to salvation are concealed from the self-sufficient and self-complacent, leaving them in nature's darkness. Third, by declaring, "and hast revealed them unto babes." By the effectual operation of the Holy Spirit a divine discovery is made by those who are helpless in their own esteem. "Even so, Father; for so it seemed good in thy sight," expressed the Savior's perfect acquiescence.

"All things are delivered unto me of my Father: and no man knoweth the Son, but the Father; neither knoweth any man the Father, save the Son, and he to whomsoever the Son will reveal him" (Matthew 11:27). This verse supplies the immediate connecting-link between the sovereignty of divine grace mentioned (vv. 25-26) and the communication of that grace through Christ (vv. 28-30). The settlements of divine grace were made and secured in the everlasting covenant; communication of it is by and through Christ as the Mediator of that covenant. First, here is the grand commission the Mediator received from the Father: all things necessary to the administration of the covenant were delivered unto Christ (cf. Matthew 28:18; John 5:22, 17:2). Second, here is the inconceivable dignity of the Son: lest a false inference be drawn from the preceding clause, the essential and absolute deity of Christ is affirmed. Inferior in office, Christ's nature and dignity is the same as the Father's. As Mediator, Christ receives all from the Father, but as God the Son He is, in every way, equal to the Father in His incomprehensible Person.

Third, here the work of the Mediator is summed up in one grand item: that of revealing the Father to those given to Him.

Thus the context of Matthew 11 reveals Christ in the following characters: as the Upbraider of the impenitent; as the Pronouncer of solemn "woe" upon those who were unaffected by His mighty works; as the Announcer of the day of judgment, declaring that the punishment awaiting those who scorned gospel mercies should be more intolerable than that meted out to Sodom; as the Affirmer of the high sovereignty of God who conceals and reveals the things pertaining to salvation; as the Mediator of the covenant; as the Son coequal with the Father; and as the One by whom the Father is revealed. "Come unto me, all ye that labor and are heavy laden, and I will give you rest" (Matthew 11:28). Having examined the context of these words, so that we might the better see their connection and the particular characters in which Christ is portrayed, consider the persons addressed, the ones who were invited to the Rest-giver. This point brings some differences among commentators. Some give a narrower scope to this call of Christ, and some a wider. Note however, that all of the leading earlier expositors restricted this particular call to a special class:

He now kindly invites to Himself those whom He acknowledges to be fit for becoming His disciples. Though He is ready to reveal the Father to all, yet the great part are careless about coming to Him, because they are not affected by a conviction of their necessities. Hypocrites give themselves no concern about Christ because they are intoxicated with their own righteousness, and neither hunger nor thirst after His grace. Those who are devoted to the world set no value on a heavenly life. It would be vain therefore for Christ to invite either of these classes, and therefore He turns to the wretched and afflicted. He speaks of them as "laboring" or being under a "burden," and does not mean generally those who are oppressed with griefs and vexations, but those who are overwhelmed by their sins, who are filled with alarm at the wrath of God and are ready to sink under so weighty a burden (John Calvin).

The character of the persons invited: all that labor and are heavy laden. This is a word in season to him that is weary (Isa. 50:4). Those that complain of the burden of the ceremonial law, which was an intolerable yoke, and was made much more so by the tradition of the elders (Luke 11:46); let them come to Christ and they shall be made easy . . . But it is rather to be understood of the burden of sin, both the guilt and the power of it. All those, and those only, are invited to rest in Christ that are sensible of sin as a burden and groan under it, that are not only convicted of the evil of sin—their own sin—but are contrite in soul for it; that are really sick of sin, weary of the service of the world and the flesh, that see their state sad and dangerous by reason of sin, and are in pain and fear about it: as Ephraim (Jer. 31:18-20), the prodigal (Luke 15:17), the publican (Luke 18:13), Peter's hearers (Acts 2:37), Paul (Acts 9), the jailor (Acts 16:29-30). This is a necessary preparative for pardon and peace (Matthew Henry).

Who are the persons here invited? They are those who "labor" (the Greek expresses toil with weariness) and are "heavy laden." This must here be limited to spiritual concerns, otherwise it will take in all mankind, even the most hardened and obstinate opposers of Christ and the Gospel. Referring to the self-righteous religionists, this writer went on to say, "You avoid gross sins, you have perhaps a form of godliness. The worst you think that can be said of you is, that you employ all your thoughts and every means that will not bring you under the lash of the law, to heap up money, to join house to house and field to field; or you spend your days in a complete indolence, walking in the way of your own hearts, and looking no further: and here you will say you find pleasure, and insist on it, that you are neither weary nor heavy laden . . . then it is plain that you are not the persons whom Christ here invites to partake of His rest (John Newton).

The persons invited are not "all" the inhabitants of mankind, but with a restriction: "all ye that labor and are heavy laden," meaning not those who labor in the service of sin and Satan, are laden with iniquity and insensible of it: those are not weary of sin nor burdened with it, nor do they want or desire any rest for their souls; but such who groan, being burdened with the guilt of sin on their consciences and are pressed down with the unsupportable yoke of the Law and the load of their trespasses, and have been laboring till they are weary, in order to obtain peace of conscience and rest for their souls by the observance of these things, but in vain. These are encouraged to come to Him, lay down their burdens at His feet and look to Him, and lay hold by faith on His person, blood and righteousness (John Gill).

In more recent times many preachers have dealt with the text (Matthew 11:28) as though the Lord Jesus was issuing an indefinite invitation, regarding His terms as sufficiently general and wide in their scope to include sinners of every type. They supposed that the words, "ye that labor and are heavy laden," refer to the misery and bondage which the fall brought upon the human race, as its unhappy subjects vainly seek satisfaction in the things of time and sense, and endeavor to find happiness in the pleasures of sin. "The universal wretchedness of man is depicted on both its sides—the active and the passive forms of it" (Fausset and Brown). They are laboring for contentment by gratifying their lusts, only to add to their miseries by becoming more and more the burdened slaves of sin.

It is true the unregenerate "labor in the very fire" and they "weary themselves for very vanity" (Hab. 2:13); it is true they "labor in vain" (Jer. 51:58), and "what profit hath he that hath labored for the wind?" (Ecclesiastes 5:16). It is true they "spend money for that which is not bread," and "labor for that which satisfieth not" (Isa. 55:2), for "the eye is not satisfied with seeing, nor the ear filled with hearing" (Eccl. 1:8). It is equally true that the unregenerate are heavy laden, "a people laden with iniquity" (Isa. 1:4), yet they are totally insensible to their awful state. "The labor of the foolish wearieth every one of them, because he knoweth not how to go to the city" (Eccl. 10:15). Moreover, "The wicked are like the troubled sea, when it cannot rest, whose waters cast up mire and dirt. There is no peace, saith my God, to the wicked" (Isa. 57:20-21). They have neither peace of conscience nor rest of heart. But it is quite another matter to affirm these are the characters Christ invited to come unto Him for rest.

We prefer the view taken by the older writers. Over a century ago a latitudinarian spirit began to creep in, and even the most orthodox were often, unconsciously, affected by it. Those in the pews were more inclined to chafe against what they regarded as the "rigidity" and "narrowness" of their fathers; and those in the pulpit had to tone down those aspects of truth which were most repellent to the carnal mind, if they were to retain their popularity. Side by side with modern inventions, an increased means for travel, and the dissemination of news, came what was termed "a broader outlook" and "a more charitable spirit." Posing as an angel of light, Satan succeeded in Arminianizing many places of truth; and even where this was not accomplished, high Calvinism was whittled down to moderate Calvinism.

These are solemn facts which no student of ecclesiastical history can deny. Christendom has not fallen into its present condition all of a sudden; rather its present state is the outcome of a long and steady deterioration. The deadly poison of error was introduced here a little, there a little, with the quantity increased as less opposition came against it. As the acquiring of "converts" absorbed more and more of the attention and strength of the Church, the standard of doctrine lowered, sentiment displaced convictions, and fleshly methods were introduced. In a comparatively short time many of those sent out to "the foreign field" were rank Arminians, preaching "another gospel." This reacted upon the homeland, and soon the interpretations of Scripture given out from pulpits moved into line with the "new spirit" which had captivated Christendom.

While we do not affirm that everything modern is evil or that everything ancient was excellent, there is no doubt that the greater part of the boasted "progress" in Christendom of the nineteenth and twentieth centuries was a progress downward and not upward—away from God and not toward Him, into the darkness and not the light. Therefore we need to examine with double caution any religious views which deviate from the common teachings of the godly Reformers and Puritans. We need not be worshipers of antiquity as such, but we need to regard with suspicion those "broader" interpretations of God's Word which have become popular in recent times.

We should point out some of the reasons why we do not believe that Christ was making a broadcast invitation that was issued promiscuously to the light-headed, gay-hearted, pleasure-crazy masses which had no appetite for the Gospel and no concern for eternal interests. This call was not addressed to the godless, careless, giddy and worldly multitudes, but rather to those who were burdened with a sense of sin and longed for relief of conscience.

First, the Lord Jesus received no commission from heaven to bestow rest of soul upon all, but only upon the elect of God. "For I am come down from heaven, not to do mine own will, but the will of him that sent me. And this is the Father's will which hath sent me, that of all which he hath given me I should lose nothing, but should raise it up again at the last day" (John 6:38-39). That, necessarily, regulated all His ministry.

Second, the Lord Jesus always practiced what He preached. To His disciples He said, "Give not that which is holy unto the dogs, neither cast ye your pearls before swine, lest they trample them under their feet, and turn again and rend you" (Matthew 7:6). Can we, then, conceive of our holy Lord inviting the unconcerned to come unto Him for that which their hearts abhorred? Has He set His ministers such an example? Surely, the word He would have them press upon the pleasure-intoxicated members of our generation is, "Rejoice, O young man, in thy youth; and let thy heart cheer thee in the days of thy youth, and walk in the ways of thine heart, and in the sight of thine eyes: but know thou, that for all these things God will bring thee into judgment" (Eccl. 11:9).

Third, the immediate context is entirely out of harmony with the wider interpretation. Christ pronounced most solemn "woes" on those who despised and rejected Him (Matthew 11:20-24), drawing consolation from the sovereignty of God and thanking Him because He had hidden from the wise and prudent the things which belonged unto their eternal peace but had revealed them unto babes (vv. 25-26). It is these "babes" He invites to Himself; and we find Him presented as the One commissioned by the Father and as the Revealer of Him (v. 27).

It must not be concluded that we do not believe in an unfettered Gospel, or that we are opposed to the general offer of Christ to all who hear it. Not so. His marching orders are far too plain for any misunderstanding; his Master has bidden him "preach the Gospel to every creature," so far as Divine providence admits, and the substance of the Gospel message is that Christ died for sinners and stands ready to welcome every sinner willing to receive Him on His terms. The Lord Jesus announced the design of His incarnation in sufficiently general terms as to warrant any man truly desiring salvation to believe in Him. "I am not come to call the righteous, but sinners to repentance" (Matthew 9:13). Many are called even though but few are chosen (Matthew 20:16). The way we spell out our election is by coming to Christ as lost sinners, trusting in His blood for pardon and acceptance with God.

In his excellent sermon on these words before us, John Newton pointed out that, when David was driven into the wilderness by the rage of Saul, "every one that was in distress, and every one that was in debt, and every one that was discontented, gathered themselves unto him; and he became a captain over them" (1 Sam. 22:2). But David was despised by those who, like Nabal (1 Sam. 25:10), lived at their ease. They did not believe he should be a king over Israel, therefore they preferred the favor of Saul, whom God had rejected. Thus it was with the Lord Jesus. Though a divine person, invested with all authority, grace, and blessings—and declaring that He would be the King of all who obeyed His voice—yet the majority saw no beauty that they should desire Him, felt no need of Him, and so rejected Him. Only a few who were consciously burdened believed His Word and came to Him for rest.

What did our Lord signify when He bade all the weary and heavy laden "come unto Me?" First, it is evident that something more than a physical act or coming to hear Him preach was intended. These words were first addressed to those already in His presence. Many who attended His ministry and witnessed His miracles never came to Him in the sense intended. The same holds true today. Something more than a bare approach through the ordinances—listening to preaching, submitting to baptism, partaking of the Lord's Supper—is involved in coming to Christ. Coming to Christ in the sense He invited is a going out of the soul after Him, a desire for Him, a seeking after Him, a personal embracing and trusting Him.

Coming to Christ suggests first, and negatively, a leaving of something, for the divine promise is, "He that covereth his sins shall not prosper: but whoso confesseth and forsaketh them shall have mercy" (Prov. 28:13). Coming to Christ, then, denotes turning our backs upon the world and turning our hearts unto Him as our only Hope. It means to abandon every idol and surrender ourselves to His Lordship; it is repudiating our own righteousness and dependency, and the heart going out to Him in loving submission and trustful confidence. It is an entire going out of self with all its resolutions to cast ourselves upon His mercy; it is the will yielding itself to His authority, to be ruled by Him and to follow where He leads. In short, it is the whole soul of a self-condemned sinner turning unto a whole Christ, exercising all our faculties, responding to His claims upon us, and prepared to unreservedly trust, unfeignedly love, and devotedly serve Him.

Thus, coming to Christ is the turning of the whole soul to Him. Perhaps this calls for amplification. There are three principal faculties in the soul: the understanding, the affections, and the will. Since each of these were operative and affected by our original departure from God, so they are and must be active in our return to Christ. Of Eve it is recorded, "When the woman saw that the tree was good for food, and that it was pleasant to the eyes, and a tree to be desired to make one wise, she took of the fruit thereof" (Gen. 3:6). First, she "saw that the tree was good for food," she perceived the fact mentally, a conclusion drawn from her understanding. Second, "and that it was pleasant to the eyes." That was the response of her affections to it. Third, "and a tree to be desired to make one wise." Here was the moving of her will. "And took of the fruit thereof and did eat," was the completed action.

So it is in the sinner's coming to Christ. First there is apprehension by the understanding. The mind is enlightened and brought to see a deep need of Christ and His suitability to meet those needs. The intelligence sees He is "good for food," the Bread of life for the nourishment of our souls. Second, there is the moving of the affections. Before, we saw no beauty in Christ that we should desire Him, but now He is "pleasant to the eyes" of our souls. It is the heart turning from the love of sin to the love of holiness, from self to the Savior. Third, in coming to Christ there is an exercise of the will, for He said to those who would not receive Him, "Ye will not come to me that ye might have life" (John 5:40). This exercise of the will is a yielding of ourselves to His authority.

None will come to Christ while they remain in ignorance of Him. The understanding must accept His suitability for sinners before the mind can turn intelligently to Him as He is revealed in the Gospel. Neither can the heart come to Christ while it hates Him or is wedded to the things of time and space. The affections must be drawn out to Him. "If any man love not the Lord Jesus Christ, let him be anathema" (1 Cor. 16:22). Equally evident is it that no man will come to Christ while his will is opposed to Him: it is the enlightening of his understanding and the firing of his affections which subdues his enmity and makes the sinner willing in the day of God's power (Ps. 110:3). Observe that these exercises of the three faculties of the soul correspond in character to the threefold office of Christ: the understanding enlightened by Him as Prophet; the affections moved by His work as Priest; and the will bowing to His authority as King.

In the days on earth the Lord Jesus stooped to minister to the needs of men's bodies, and not a few came unto Him and were healed. In that we may see an adumbration of Him as the Great Physician of souls and what is required of sinners if they are to receive spiritual healing at His hand. Those who sought out Christ to obtain bodily relief were persuaded of His mighty power, His gracious willingness, and of their own dire need. But note that then, as now, this persuasion in the Lord's sufficiency and His readiness to nourish varied in different cases. The centurion spoke with full assurance, "Speak the word only, and my servant shall be healed" (Matthew 8:8). The leper expressed himself more dubiously, "Lord, if thou wilt, thou canst make me clean" (Matthew 8:2). Another used fainter language, "If thou canst do any thing, have compassion and help us" (Mark 9:22); yet even there the Redeemer did not break the bruised reed nor quench the smoking flax, but graciously wrought a miracle on his behalf.

But observe that in each of these cases there was a personal, actual application to Christ; and it was this very application which manifested their faith, even though it was as small as a grain of mustard seed. They were not content with having heard of His fame, but improved it. They sought Him out for themselves, acquainted Him with their case, and implored His compassion. So it must be with those troubled about soul concerns. Saving faith is not passive, but operative. Moreover, the faith of those who sought Christ for physical relief refused to be deterred by difficulties. In vain the multitudes charged the blind man to be quiet (Mark 10:48). Knowing that Christ was able to give sight, he cried so much the more. Even when Christ appeared to manifest a great reserve, the woman refused to leave till her request was granted (Matthew 15:27).

CHAPTER 16
The Rest of Christ

"Come unto Me, all ye that labor and are heavy laden, and I will give you rest" (Matthew 11:28). In a message on these words John Newton pointed out: The dispensation of the Gospel may be compared to the cities of refuge in Israel. It was a privilege and honor to the nation in general that they had such sanctuaries of Divine appointment, but the real value of them was known and felt by only a few. Those alone who found themselves in that case for which they were provided could rightly prize them. Thus it is with the Gospel of Christ: it is the highest privilege and honor of which a professing nation can boast, but it can be truly understood and esteemed by none except weary and heavy laden souls, who have felt their misery by nature, are tired of the drudgery of sin, and have seen the broken Law pursuing them like the avenger of blood of old. This is the only consideration which keeps them from sinking into abject despair, in that God has graciously provided a remedy by the Gospel and that Christ bids them "Come unto Me, and I will give you rest."

If awakened, convicted, and distressed souls would but appropriate the full comfort of that blessed invitation and obey its terms, their complaints would end; but remaining ignorance, the workings of unbelief, and the opposition of Satan combine to keep them back. Some will say, "I am not qualified to come to Christ: my heart is so hard, my conscience so insensible, that I do not feel the burden of my sins as I ought, nor my need of Christ's rest as I should." Others will say, "I fear that I do not come aright. I see from the Scriptures and hear from the pulpit that repentance is required from me and that faith is an absolute essential if I am to be saved; but I am concerned to know whether my repentance is sincere and deep enough and if my faith is anything better than an historical one—the assent of the mind to the facts in the Gospel."

We may discover from those who sought healing from Him what is meant by the invitation Christ makes to those who have sought the approval of God and met His requirements in the Law. First, they were persuaded of His power and willingness and of their own deep need of His help. So it is in the matter of salvation. The sinner must be convinced that Christ is "mighty to save," that He is ready to receive all who are sick of sin and want to be healed. Second, they made an application to Him. They were not content to hear of His fame, but wanted proof of His wonderworking power. So too the sinner must not only credit the message of the Gospel, but also he must seek Him and trust Him.

Those who sought Christ as a Physician of souls continued with Him and became His followers. They received Him as their Lord and Master, renounced what was inconsistent with His will (Luke 9:23, 60), professed an obedience to His precepts, and accepted a share in His reproach. Some had a more definite call to Him, such as Matthew, who was sitting at the receipt of custom, indifferent to the claims of Christ until He said, "Follow me" (Matthew 9:9). That word was accompanied with power and won his heart, separating him from worldly pursuits in an instant. Others were drawn to Him more secretly by His Spirit, such as Nathanael (John 1:46), and the weeping penitent (Luke 7:38). The ruler came to the Lord with no other intention than to obtain the life of his son (John 4:53), but he secured much more than he expected, and he believed, with all his house.

These things are recorded for our encouragement. The Lord Jesus is not on earth in visible form, but He promised His spiritual presence to abide with His Word, His ministers, and His people to the end. Weary sinners do not have to take a hard journey to find the Savior, for He is always near (Acts 17:27) wherever His Gospel is preached. "But the righteousness which is of faith speaketh on this wise, Say not in thine heart, Who shall ascend into heaven? (That is, to bring Christ down from above.) Or, Who shall descend into the deep? (That is, to bring up Christ again from the dead.) But what saith it? The word is nigh thee, even in thy mouth, and in thy heart: that is, the word of faith, which we preach" (Rom. 10:6-8). If you cannot come to Christ with a tender heart and burdened conscience, then come to Him for them.

Is it a sense of your load which makes you say you are not able? Then consider that this is not a work, but a rest. Would a man plead I am so heavy laden that I cannot consent to part with my burden; so weary that I am not able either to stand still or to lie down, but must force myself farther? The greatness of your burden, so far from being an objection, is the very reason why you should instantly come to Christ, for He alone is able to release you. But perhaps you think you do not come aright. I ask, how would you come? If you come as a helpless unworthy sinner, without righteousness, without any hope but what arises from the worth, work, and Word of Christ, this is to come aright. There is no other way of being accepted. Would you refresh and strengthen yourself, wash away your own sins, free yourself from your burden, and then come to Him to do these things for you? May the Lord help you to see the folly and unreasonableness of your unbelief (John Newton).

There is no promise in Scripture that God will reward the careless, halfhearted, indolent seeker; but He has declared, "Ye shall seek me, and find me, when ye shall search for me with all your heart" (Jer. 29:13) He has a fixed time for everyone whom He receives. He knew how long the poor man had waited at the pool (John 5:6), and when His hour came He healed him. So endeavor to be found in the way: where His Word is preached, and diligently search His Word in the privacy of your room. Be much in prayer. Converse with His people, and He may join you unexpectedly, as He did the two disciples walking to Emmaus.

"I will give you rest." What a claim! No mere man, no matter how godly and spiritual, could promise this. Abraham, Moses, or David could not bid the weary and heavy laden to come unto him with the assurance that he would give them rest. To impart rest of soul to another is beyond the power of the most exalted creature. Even the holy angels are incapable of bestowing rest upon others, for they are dependent on the grace of God for their own rest. Thus this promise of Christ manifested His uniqueness. Neither Confucius, Buddha, nor Mohammed ever made such a claim. It was no mere Man who uttered these words, "Come unto me all ye that are weary and heavy laden, and I will give you rest." He was the Son of God. He made man, and therefore He could restore him. He was the Prince of peace, thus capable of giving rest.

As Christ is the only One who can bestow rest of soul, so there is no true rest apart from Him. The creature cannot impart it. The world cannot communicate it. We cannot manufacture it. One of the most pathetic things in the world is to see the unregenerate vainly seek happiness and contentment in the material things. At last they discover these are all broken cisterns which hold no water. Observe them turning to priests or preachers, penance or fastings, reading and praying, only to find, as the prodigal son did when he "began to be in want," that "no man gave unto him" (Luke 15); or see the poor woman who had "suffered many things of many physicians, and had spent all that she had, and was nothing bettered, but rather grew worse" (Mark 5:26). All the unregenerate, illiterate or learned, find "the way of peace have they not known" (Rom. 3:17).

It is much to be thankful for when we realize experimentally that none but Christ can do helpless sinners any good. This is a hard lesson for man, and we are slow to learn it. The fact is not involved in itself, but the devilish pride of our hearts makes us self-sufficient until divine grace humbles us. It is part of the gracious work of the Holy Spirit to bring us off our creature dependence, to knock the props from under us, to make us see that Jesus Christ is our only hope. "Neither is there salvation in any other: for there is none other name under heaven given among men, whereby we must be saved" (Acts 4:12). Strikingly this was illustrated by the dove sent forth by Noah. "But the dove found no rest for the sole of her foot, and she returned unto him into the ark, for the waters were on the face of the whole earth: then he put forth his hand, and took her, and pulled her in unto him into the ark" (Gen. 8:9). Significantly, the very name "Noah" meant "rest" (Gen. 5:29, margin); and it was only as the dove was "caused to come unto him" that she obtained rest. So it is with the sinner.

What is the nature of this rest Christ gives to all who come to Him?

The Greek word expresses something more than rest, or a mere relaxation from toil; it denotes refreshment likewise. A person weary with long bearing a heavy burden will need not only to have it removed, but likewise he wants food and refreshment to restore his spirits and to repair his wasted strength. Such is the rest of the Gospel. It not only puts a period to our fruitless labor, but it affords a sweet reviving cordial. There is not only peace, but joy in believing (John Newton).

Thus it is a spiritual rest, a satisfying rest, "rest for the soul" as the Savior declares in this passage. It is such a rest the world can neither give nor take away.

In particularizing upon the nature of this rest we may distinguish between its present and future forms. Concerning the former, First, it is a deliverance from that vain and wearisome quest which absorbs the sinner before the Spirit opens his eyes to see his folly and moves him to seek true riches. Piteous it is to behold those who are made for eternity wasting their energies in wandering from object to object, searching for what will not satisfy, only to be mortified by repeated disappointments. It is so with all until they come to Christ, for He has written about all the pleasures of this world, "Whosoever drinketh of this water shall thirst again" (John 4:13). For example, Solomon, who had everything the heart could desire and gratified his lusts to the full, found that, "behold, all is vanity and vexation of spirit" (Eccl. 1:14). From this vexation of spirit Christ delivers His people, for He declares, "whosoever drinketh of the water that I shall give him shall never thirst" (John 4:14).

Second, it is the easing and tranquilizing of a burdened conscience. Only one who has been convicted by the Holy Spirit appreciates what this means. When one has to cry out, "The arrows of the Almighty are within me, the poison whereof drinketh up my spirit: the terrors of God do set themselves in array against me" (Job 6:4); when the curse of God's broken Law thunders in our ears; when we have an inward sense of divine wrath and the terrors of a future judgment fall upon the soul, then there is indescribable anguish of mind. When a true work is wrought in the heart by the Spirit we exclaim, "Thine arrows stick fast in me, and thy hand presseth me sore. There is no soundness in my flesh because of thine anger; neither is there any rest in my bones because of my sin" (Ps. 38:2-3). When we first see the wondrous love of God for us, and how vilely we have repaid Him, then we are cut to the quick. When by faith we come to Christ all this is altered. As we see Him dying in our stead and that there is now no condemnation for us, the intolerable load falls from our conscience—and a peace which passeth all understanding is ours.

Third, it is a rest from the dominion and power of sin. Here again only those who are the subjects of His grace can enter into what is meant. The unawakened are unconcerned about the glory of God, indifferent as to whether their conduct pleases Him. They have no concept of the sinfulness of sin and no realization of how completely sin dominates them. Only when the Spirit of God illumines their minds and convicts their consciences do they see the awfulness of their state; and only then, as they try to reform their ways, are they conscious of the might of their inward foe and of their inability to cope with him. In vain deliverance is sought in resolutions and endeavors in our own strength. Even after we are quickened and begin to understand the Gospel, for a season (often a lengthy one) it is rather a fight than a rest. But as we grow more out of ourselves and are taught to live in Christ and draw our strength from Him by faith, we obtain a rest in this respect also.

Fourth, there is a rest from our own works. As the believer realizes more clearly the sufficiency of the finished work of Christ he is delivered experimentally from the Law and sees that he no longer owes it service. His obedience is no longer legal but evangelical, no longer out of fear, but out of gratitude. His service to the Lord is not in a servile, but in a gracious spirit. What was formerly a burden is now a delight. He no longer seeks to earn God's favor, but acts in the realization that the smile of God is upon him. Far from rendering him careless, this will spur him on to strive to glorify the One who gave His own Son as a sacrifice. Thus, bondage gives place to liberty, slavery to sonship, toil to rest. And the soul reposes on the unchangeable Word of Christ and follows Him steadily through light and darkness.

There is also a future rest beyond any that can be experienced here, although our best conceptions of the glory awaiting the people of God are inadequate. First, in heaven there will be a perfect resting from all sin, for nothing shall enter there which could defile or disturb our peace. What it will mean to be delivered from indwelling corruptions no tongue can tell. The closer a believer walks with the Lord, and the more intimate his communion with Him is, the more bitterly he hates that within him which ever fights against his desire for holiness. Therefore the apostle cried, "O wretched man that I am! who shall deliver me from the body of this death?" (Rom. 7:24). But we will not carry this burden beyond the grave.

Second, we shall be delivered from beholding the sins of others. No more will our hearts be pained by the evils which flood the earth. Like Lot in Sodom, we are grieved with the conversation of the godless. "Who that has any love to the Lord Jesus, any spark of true holiness, any sense of the worth of souls in his heart, can see what passes amongst us without trembling? How openly, daringly, almost universally, are the commandments of God broken, His Gospel despised, His patience abused, and His power defied" (John Newton). If that were the state of affairs 200 years ago what would this writer say were he on earth today to witness not only the wickedness of a profane world, but also the hypocrisy of Christendom? As the believer sees how the Lord is dishonored in the house of those who pose as His friends, how often he thinks, "Oh that I had wings like a dove! for then would I fly away, and be at rest" (Ps. 55:6).

Third, there will be perpetual rest from all outward afflictions; for in heaven none will harass the people of God. No more will the saint live in the midst of an ungodly generation, which may not actively persecute him, yet they only reluctantly tolerate his presence. Though afflictions are needful, and when sanctified to us are also profitable, nevertheless they are grievous to bear. But a day is coming when these tribulations will no longer be necessary, for the fine gold will have been purged from the dross. The storms of life will be behind, and an unbroken calm will be the believer's lot forever. Where there will be no more sin, there will be no more sorrow. "God shall wipe away all tears from their eyes; and there shall be no more death, neither sorrow, nor crying, neither shall there be any more pain: for the former things are passed away" (Rev. 21:4).

Fourth, it will be a rest from Satan's temptations. How often he disturbs the present rest of believers! How often they have cause to say with the apostle, "Satan hath hindered me." He seeks in various ways to hinder them from attending the public means of grace; to hinder them when they try to meditate on the Word or pray. The devil cannot bear to see one of Christ's people happy, so he tries constantly to disturb their joy. One reason why God permits this is that they may be conformed to their Head. When He was here on earth the devil continually hounded Him. Even when believers come to the hour of departure from this world, their great enemy seeks to rob them of assurance, but he can pursue them no further. Absent from the body, they are present with the Lord, forever out of the reach of their adversary.

Finally, they rest from unsatisfied desires. When one has really been born of the Spirit, he wants to be done with sin forever. He longs for perfect conformity to the image of Christ, and for unbroken fellowship with Him. But such longings are not realized in this life. Instead, the old nature within the believer ever opposes the new, bringing him into captivity to the law of sin (Rom. 7:23). But death affords final relief from indwelling corruptions, and he is made "a pillar in the temple of his God, and he shall go out no more" (Rev. 3:12). On the morning of the resurrection the believer's body shall be "fashioned like unto his glorious body" (Phil. 3:21), and his soul's every longing shall then be fully realized. The change from grace to glory will be as radical as the change from nature to grace.

CHAPTER 17
The Yoke of Christ

"Come unto Me all ye that labor and are heavy laden, and I will give you rest." This is not a broadcast invitation, addressed indefinitely to the careless, giddy masses; rather is it a gracious call to those who seriously seek peace of heart, yet are still bowed down with a load of guilt. It is addressed to those who long for rest of soul, but who know not how it is to be obtained, nor where it is to be found. To such Christ says, "Come unto me, and I will give you rest." But He does not leave it there. He goes on to explain. Our Lord makes the bare affirmation that He is the giver of rest (Matthew 11:28). In what follows He specifies the terms on which He dispenses it, conditions which we must meet if we are to obtain it. The rest is freely "given," but only to those who comply with the revealed requirements of its Bestower.

"Take my yoke upon you and learn of me; for I am meek and lowly in heart; and ye shall find rest unto your souls" (Matthew 11:29). In those words Christ voiced the conditions which men must meet if they are to obtain rest of soul. We are required to take His yoke upon us. The yoke is a figure of subjection. The force of this figure may be understood if we contrast oxen running wild in the field with oxen harnessed to a plow, where their owner directs their energies. Hence we read, "It is good for a man that he bear the yoke in his youth" (Lam. 3:27). That means unless youths are disciplined, brought under subjection and taught to obey their superiors, they are likely to develop into sons of Belial, intractable rebels against God and man. When the Lord took Ephraim in hand and chastised him, he bemoaned that he was like "a bullock unaccustomed to the yoke" (Jer. 31:18).

The natural man is born "like a wild ass's colt" (Job 11:12)—completely unmanageable, self-willed, determined to have his own way at all costs. Having lost his anchor by the fall, man is like a ship entirely at the mercy of winds and waves. His heart is unmoored and he runs wild to his own destruction. Thus he has a need for the yoke of Christ if he is to obtain rest for his soul. In its larger sense, the yoke of Christ signifies complete dependence, unqualified obedience, unreserved submission to Him. The believer owes this to Christ both as his rightful Lord and his gracious Redeemer. Christ has a double claim upon him: he is the creature of His hands, and gave him being, with all his capacities and faculties. He has redeemed him and acquired an additional claim on him. The saints are the purchased property of another; therefore the Holy Spirit says, "Ye are not your own, for ye are bought with a price: therefore glorify God in your body, and in your spirit, which are God's (1 Cor. 6:19-20).

"Take my yoke upon you," by which Christ meant: surrender yourself to My Lordship, submit to My rule, let My will be yours. As Matthew Henry pointed out: We are here invited to Christ as Prophet, Priest and King, to be saved, and in order to this, to be ruled and taught by Him. As the oxen are yoked in order to submit to their owner's will and to work under his control, so those who would receive rest of soul from Christ are here called upon to yield to Him as their King. He died for His people that they should not henceforth live unto themselves, "but unto him which died for them, and rose again" (2 Cor. 5:15). Our holy Lord requires absolute submission and obedience in all things both in the inward life and the outward, even to "bringing into captivity every thought to the obedience of Christ" (2 Cor. 10:5). Alas that this is so little insisted upon in a day when the high claims of the Savior are whittled down in an attempt to render His Gospel more acceptable to the unregenerate.

It was different in the past, when those in the pulpit kept back nothing profitable for their hearers. God honored such faithful preaching by granting the anointing of His Spirit, so that the Word was applied in power. Take this sample: No heart can truly open to Christ that is not made willing, upon due deliberation, to receive Him with His cross of sufferings and His yoke of obedience: "If any man will come after me, let him deny himself, and take up his cross, and follow me . . . Take my yoke upon you, and learn of me" (Matthew 16:24; 11:29). Any exception against either of these is an effectual barrier to union with Christ. He looks upon that soul as not worthy of Him that puts in such an exception: "he that taketh not his cross, and followeth after me, is not worthy of me" (Matthew 10:38). If thou judgeth not Christ to be worthy all sufferings, all losses, all reproaches, He judges thee unworthy to bear the name of His disciple. So, for the duties of obedience—called His "yoke"—he that will not receive Christ's yoke can neither receive His pardon nor any benefit by His blood (John Flavel, 1689).

"Take my yoke upon you." Note carefully that the yoke is not laid upon us by another, but one which we place upon ourselves. It is a definite act on the part of one who seeks rest from Christ, and without which His rest cannot be obtained. It is a specific act of mind, an act of conscious surrender to His authority, to be ruled only by Him. Saul took this yoke upon him when, convicted of his rebellion and conquered by a sense of the Savior's compassion, he said, "Lord, what wouldest thou have me to do?" To take Christ's yoke upon us signifies setting aside of our wills and completely submitting to His sovereignty, acknowledging His Lordship in a practical way. Christ demands something more than lip service from His followers, even a loving obedience to all His commands, "Not every one that saith unto me, Lord, Lord, shall enter into the kingdom of heaven; but he that doeth the will of my Father which is in heaven . . . "whosoever heareth these sayings of mine, and doeth them, I will liken him unto a wise man, which built his house upon a rock" (Matthew 7:21, 24).

"Take my yoke upon you." Our coming to Christ necessarily implies turning of our backs upon all that is opposed to Him. "Let the wicked forsake his way, and the unrighteous man his thoughts: and let him return unto the LORD, and he will have mercy upon him" (Isa. 55:7). So taking His yoke presupposes our throwing off the yoke we had worn before, the yoke of sin and Satan, of self-will and self-pleasing. "O LORD our God, other lords besides thee have had dominion over us" confessed Israel of old (Isa. 26:13). Then they added, "but by thee only will we make mention of thy name." Thus taking Christ's yoke upon us denotes a change of master, a conscious, cheerful change on our part. "Neither yield ye your members as instruments of unrighteousness unto sin . . . Know ye not, that to whom ye yield yourselves servants to obey, his servants ye are to whom ye obey: whether of sin unto death or of obedience unto righteousness" (Rom. 6:13, 16).

"Take my yoke upon you." It may sound much like a paradox—to bid those who labor and are heavy laden, who come to Christ for "rest," to take a "yoke" upon them. Yet, in reality it is far from the case. Instead of the yoke of Christ bringing its wearer into bondage, it introduces a real liberty, the only genuine liberty there is. The Lord Jesus said to those who believed in Him, "If ye continue in my word, then are ye my disciples indeed; and ye shall know the truth, and the truth shall make you free" (John 8:31-32). There must first be a "continuing in His Word," a constant walking in it. As we do this He makes good His promise, "and ye shall know the Truth": know it in an experimental way, know its power, and its blessedness. The consequence is, "the Truth shall make you free"—free from prejudice, from ignorance, from folly, from self-will, from the grievous bondage of Satan and the power of sin. Then the obedient disciple discovers that divine commandments are "the perfect law of liberty" (James 1:25). David said, "I will walk at liberty: for I seek thy precepts" (Ps. 119:45).

By the yoke, two oxen were united together in the plow. The yoke then is a figure of practical union. This is clear from, "Be ye not unequally yoked together with unbelievers: for what fellowship hath righteousness with unrighteousness? and what communion hath light with darkness? (2 Cor. 6:14). The Lord's people are forbidden to enter into any intimate relationships with unbelievers, prohibited from marrying, forming business partnerships, or having any religious union with them. This yoke speaks of a union which results in a close communion. Christ invites those who come to Him for rest to enter into a practical union with Him so that they may enjoy fellowship together. So it was with Enoch, who "walked with God" (Gen. 5:24). But "Can two walk together except they be agreed?" (Amos 3:3). They cannot. They must be joined together in aim and unity of purpose, to glorify God.

"Take my yoke upon you." He does not ask us to wear something He has not worn. O the wonder of this! "Let this mind be in you, which was also in Christ Jesus: who, being in the form of God, thought it not robbery to be equal with God; but made himself of no reputation, and took upon him the form of a servant, and was made in the likeness of men: and being found in fashion as a man, he humbled himself, and became obedient unto death, even the death of the cross" (Phil. 2:5-8). The One who was equal with God "made himself of no reputation." He, the Lord of glory, took upon Him "the form of a servant." The very Son of God was "made of a woman, made under the law" (Gal. 4:4). "Even Christ pleased not himself" (Rom. 15:3); "I came down from heaven, not to do mine own will, but the will of him that sent me" (John 6:38). This was the yoke to which He gladly submitted, complete subjection to the Father's will, loving obedience to His commands. And here He says, "Take my yoke upon you." Do as I did, making God's will yours. John Newton pointed out this is three-fold:

First, the yoke of His profession, putting on of the Christian uniform and owning the banner of our Commander. This is no irksome duty, rather is it a delight. Those who have tasted that the Lord is gracious are far from being ashamed of Him and of His Gospel. They want to tell all who will hear what God has done for their souls. It was true of Andrew and Philip (John 1:41, 43), and with the woman of Samaria (John 4:28-29). As someone has said, "Many young converts in the first warmth of their affection have more need of a bridle than of a spur in this concern." No Christian should ever be afraid to show his colors; nevertheless he should not flaunt them before those who detest them. We will not go far wrong if we heed, "Be ready always to give an answer to every man that asketh you a reason of the hope that is in you with meekness and fear" (1 Pet. 3:15). It is only when, like Peter, we follow Christ "afar off," that we are in danger of denying our discipleship.

Second, the yoke of His precepts. These the gracious soul approves and delights in: but still we are renewed but in part. And when the commands of Christ stand in direct opposition to the will of man, or call upon us to sacrifice a right hand or a right eye; though the Lord will surely make those who depend upon Him victorious at the last, yet it will cost them a struggle; so that, when they are sensible how much they owe to His power working in them, and enabling them to overcome, they will, at the same time, have a lively conviction of their own weakness. Abraham believed in God, and delighted to obey, yet when he was commanded to sacrifice his only son, this was no easy trial of his sincerity and obedience; and all who are partakers of his faith are exposed to meet, sooner or later, with some call of duty little less contrary to the dictates of flesh and blood (John Newton).

Third, the yoke of His dispensations, His dealings with us in Providence. If we enjoy the favor of the Lord, it is certain that we will be out of favor with those who hate Him. He has plainly warned, "If ye were of the world, the world would love his own: but because ye are not of the world, but I have chosen you out of the world, therefore the world hateth you" (John 15:19). It is useless to suppose that, by acting prudently and circumspectly, we can avoid this. "All that will live godly in Christ Jesus shall suffer persecution" (2 Tim. 3:12). It is only by unfaithfulness, by hiding our light under a bushel, by compromising the Truth, by attempting to serve two masters, that we can escape "the reproach of Christ." He was hated by the world and has called us to fellowship with His sufferings. This is part of the yoke He requires His disciples to bear. Moreover, "whom the Lord loveth he chasteneth." It is hard to bear the opposition of the world, but it is harder still to endure the rod of the Lord. The flesh is still in us and resists vigorously when our wills are crossed; nevertheless we are gradually taught to say with Christ, "the cup which my Father hath given me, shall I not drink it?" (John 18:11).

"And learn of me: for I am meek and lowly in heart." Once again we call attention to the deep importance of observing our Lord's order here. Just as there can be no taking of His yoke upon us until we "come" to Him, so there is no learning of Him (in the sense meant) until we have taken His yoke upon us—until we have surrendered our wills to His and submitted to His authority. This is far more than an intellectual learning of Christ, it is an experimental, effectual, transforming learning. By painstaking effort any man may acquire a theological knowledge of the person and doctrine of Christ. He may even obtain a clear concept of His meekness and lowliness; but that is vastly different from learning of Him in so as to be "changed into the same image from glory to glory" (2 Cor. 3:18). To "learn" of Him we must be completely subject to Him and in close communion with Him.

What is it that we most need to be taught of Him? How to do what will make us objects of admiration in the religious world? Or how to obtain such wisdom that we will be able to solve all mysteries? How to accomplish such great things that we will be given the preeminence among our brethren? No indeed, nothing resembling these, for "that which is highly esteemed among men is abomination in the sight of God" (Luke 16:15). What, then, Lord? This: "Learn of me, for I am meek and lowly in heart." These are the graces we most need to cultivate, the fruits which the Husbandman most highly values. Of the former grace it is said, "even the ornament of a meek and quiet spirit, which in the sight of God is of great price" (1 Pet. 3:4); of the latter the Lord declared, "I dwell in the high and holy place, with him also that is of a contrite and humble spirit" (Isa. 57:15). Do we really believe these Scriptures?

"For I am meek." What is meekness? We may best discover the answer by observing the word in other verses. For example, "Now the man Moses was very meek, above all the men which were upon the face of the earth" (Num. 12:3). This refers to the gentleness of Moses' spirit under unjust opposition. Instead of returning evil, he prayed for the healing of Miriam. So far from being weakness (as the world supposes), meekness is the strength of the man who can rule his own spirit under provocation, subduing his resentment of wrong, and refusing to retaliate. The "meek and quiet spirit" also has to do with the subjection of a wife to her husband (1 Pet. 3:1-6); her chaste conversation (or behavior) which is to be "coupled with fear" (v. 2); even as Sarah "obeyed Abraham, calling him lord" (v. 6). It is inseparably associated with gentleness: "the meekness and gentleness of Christ" (2 Cor. 10:1); "gentle, shewing all meekness unto all men" (Titus 3:2). The "spirit of meekness" is in sharp contrast from the apostle using "the rod" (1 Cor. 4:21).

Thus we may say that "meekness" is the opposite of self-will. It is pliability, yieldedness, offering no resistance, as clay in the Potter's hands. When the Maker of heaven and earth exclaimed, "I am a worm, and no man" (Ps. 22:6), He referred not only to the unparalleled depths of shame into which He descended for our sakes, but also to His lowliness and submission to the Father's will. A worm has no power of resistance, not even when it is stepped on. So there was nothing in the perfect Servant which opposed the will of God. Behold in Him the majesty of meekness, when He stood like a lamb before her shearers, committing Himself to the righteous Judge. Contrast Satan, who is represented as "the great red dragon"; while the Lamb stands as the symbol of the meekest and gentlest.

The meekness of Christ appeared in His readiness to become the covenant head of His people, and to assume our nature; in being subject to His parents during the days of His childhood; in submitting to the ordinance of baptism; in His entire subjection to the Father's will. He made no retaliation; He counted not His life dear unto Himself, but freely laid it down for others. We most need to learn of Him not how to become great or self-important, but how to deny self, to become tractable and gentle, to be servants—not only His servants, but also the servants of our brethren.

"For I am meek and lowly in heart." As meekness is the opposite of self-will, so lowliness is the reverse of self-esteem and self-righteousness. Lowliness is self-abasement, yes, self-effacement. It is more than a refusing to stand up for our own rights. Though He was so great a Person, this grace was preeminently displayed by Christ. "The Son of man came not to be ministered unto, but to minister" (Matthew 20:28); "I am among you as he that serveth" (Luke 22:27). Behold Him as he performed the menial duties of washing: the feet of His disciples. He was the only one born into this world who could choose the home and the circumstances of His birth. What a rebuke to our foolish pride His choice was! My reader, we must indeed learn of Him if this choice flower of paradise is to bloom in the garden of our souls.

CHAPTER 18
The Quintessence of Christ

The Lord Jesus uttered a gracious invitation which is accompanied by a precious promise—"Come unto me, all ye that labor and are heavy laden, and I will give you rest. Take my yoke upon you, and learn of me; for I am meek and lowly in heart: and ye shall find rest unto your souls" (Matthew 11:28-29)—and then He proceeded to make known the conditions of that promise. To those whose consciences are weighted down by a burden of guilt and who are anxious for relief, He says, "Come unto me and rest." But His rest can only be obtained as we meet His requirements: that we take His "yoke" upon us, and that we "learn" of Him. Taking Christ's yoke upon us consists of surrendering our wills to Him, submitting to His authority, consenting to be ruled by Him (see chapter 42). Now consider what it means to "learn" of Him.

Christ is the antitypical Prophet, to whom all of the Old Testament prophets pointed. He alone was personally qualified to fully make known the will of God. "God, who at sundry times and in diverse manners spake in time past unto the fathers, by the prophets, hath in these last days spoken unto us by his Son" (Heb. 1:1-2). Christ is the grand Teacher of His Church, all others are subordinate to and appointed by Him. "He gave some, apostles; and some, prophets: and some evangelists; and some, pastors and teachers; for the perfecting of the saints, for the work of the ministry, for the edifying of the body of Christ" (Eph. 4:11-12). Christ is the chief Shepherd and Feeder of His flock, His undershepherds learn of and receive from Him. Christ is the personal Word in whom and through whom the divine perfections are illustriously displayed. "No man hath seen God at any time; the only begotten Son, which is in the bosom of the Father, he hath declared him" (John 1:18). So we must come to Christ to be instructed in heavenly doctrine and built up in our holy faith.

"Learn of me." Christ is not only the final Spokesman of God, the One by whom the divine will is fully uttered, but also He is also the grand Exemplar set before His people. Christ did more than proclaim the Truth, He became the embodiment of it. He did more than utter the will of God; He was the personal exemplification of it. The divine requirements were perfectly set forth in the character and conduct of the Lord Jesus. And therein He differed radically from all who went before Him, and all who come after Him. The lives of the prophets (Old Testament) and the apostles (New Testament) shed scattered rays of light, but they were merely reflections of the Light. Christ is "the Sun of righteousness,'' therefore fully qualified to say, "learn of me." There was no error in His teaching, nor the slightest blemish in His character, or flaw in His conduct. The life He lived presents to us a perfect standard of holiness, a perfect pattern for us to follow.

When His enemies asked, "Who art thou?" He answered, "even the same that I said unto you from the beginning" (John 8:25). The force of that remarkable answer (expressed in the Greek) is brought out yet more plainly in Bagster's Interlinear and the margin of the American Revised Version, "Altogether that which I also spoke unto thee." In reply to their interrogation, the Son of God affirmed that He was essentially and absolutely what He declared Himself to be. I have spoken of "light"; I am that light. I have spoken of "truth", I am that truth—the incarnation, personification, and exemplification thereof. None but He could really say I am Myself what I am speaking to you about. The child of God may speak the truth and walk in the truth, but He is not the truth. Christ is! A Christian may let his light shine, but he is not the light. Christ was, and therein we see His exalted uniqueness. "We may know him that is true" (1 John 5:20); not "him who taught the truth," but "him that is true."

Because the Lord Jesus could make this claim—"I am altogether that which I spoke unto thee": I am the living embodiment, the personal exemplification of all which I teach, that He is a perfect Pattern for us to follow—that He can say, "Learn of me." "He has left us an example, that we should follow His steps" (1 Pet. 2:21). Since we bear His name (Christians) we should imitate His holiness. "Be ye followers of me, as I also am of Christ" (1 Cor. 11:1). The best of men are but men at the best. They have their errors and defects, which they freely acknowledge; therefore where they differ from Christ it is our duty to differ from them. No man, however wise or holy, is a perfect rule for other men. The standard of perfection is in Christ alone; He is the rule of every Christian's walk. "Not as though I had already attained, either were already perfect: but I follow after, if that I may apprehend that for which also I am apprehended of Christ Jesus" (Phil. 3:12). Though we fall far short of teaching such a standard in this life, nothing short of it should be our aim.

"He that saith he abideth in him ought himself also so to walk even as he walked" (1 John 2:6). Many reasons might be given in proof of "ought." It is vain for any man to profess he is a Christian unless he evidences that it is both his desire and endeavor to follow the example Christ left His people. As the Puritans said, "Let him either put on the life of Christ, or put off the name of Christ; let him show the hand of a Christian in works of holiness and obedience, or else the tongue and language of a Christian must gain no belief or credit." God has predestinated His people "to be conformed to the image of his Son" (Rom. 8:29). The work was begun here and perfected after death, but that work is not consummated in heaven unless it is commenced on earth. "We may as well hope to be saved without Christ, as to be saved without conformity to Christ" (John Flavel).

This practical conformity between God's Son and His sons is indispensable to their relation in grace, this relationship between body and head. Believers are members of a living organism of which Christ is the Head; of members, "By one Spirit we are all baptized into one body, whether we be Jews or Gentiles, whether we be bond or free; and have been all made to drink into one Spirit" (1 Cor. 12:13); of Christ, "and [God] gave him to be the head over all things to the church, which is his body, the fullness of him that filleth all in all" (Eph. 1:22-23). The two together (members and Head) form Christ-mystical. Now as Christ, the Head, is pure and holy, so also must be the members. An animal with a human head would be a monstrosity. For the sensual and godless to claim oneness to Christ is to misrepresent Him before the world, as though His mystical Body were like the image of Nebuchadnezzar, with the head of fine gold and the feet of iron and clay (Dan. 2:32 ff.).

This resemblance to Christ appears necessary from the communion which all believers have with Him in the same Spirit of grace and holiness. Christ is the "Firstborn among many brethren," and God anointed Him "with the oil of gladness above thy fellows" (Ps. 45:7). That oil of gladness is an emblem of the Holy Spirit, and God gives the same to each of the fellows or partners. Where the same Spirit and principle is, there the same fruits and works must be produced, according to the proportions of the Spirit of grace bestowed. This is the very reason the Holy Spirit is given to believers. "But we all, with open face beholding as in a glass the glory of the Lord, are changed into the same image from glory to glory, even as by the Spirit of the Lord" (2 Cor. 3:18).

Also, the very honor of Christ demands conformity of Christians to His example. In what other way can they close the mouths of those who reject their Master and vindicate His blessed name from the reproaches of the world? How can Wisdom be justified of her children except in this way? The wicked will not read the inspired record of His life in the Scriptures; therefore there is all the more need to have His excellencies set before them in the lives of His people. The world sees what we practice, as well as hears what we profess. Unless there is consistency between our profession and practice we cannot glorify Christ before a world which has cast Him out.

Then, there must be an inward conformity to Christ before there can be any resemblance on the outside. There must be an experimental oneness before there can be a practical likeness. How can we possibly be conformed to Him in external acts of obedience unless we are conformed to Him in those springs from which such actions proceed? We must live in the Spirit before we can walk in the Spirit (Gal. 5:25). "Let this mind be in you, which was also in Christ Jesus" (Phil. 2:5), for the mind should regulate all our other faculties. Therefore we are told, "For to be carnally minded is death; but to be spiritually minded is life and peace" (Rom. 8:6). What was "the mind which was in Christ Jesus?" It was that of self-abnegation and devotedness to the Father. That we must begin with inward conformity to Christ is evident from our text; after saying "learn of me." He at once added, "for I am meek and lowly in heart."

We need to attend closely to our Lord's order in this passage, insisting we cannot possibly "learn" of Him (in the sense meant here) until we have taken His "yoke" upon us, until we surrender ourselves to Him. It is not merely to an intellectual learning of Him which Christ calls us, but to an experimental, effectual, and transforming learning; and in order to obtain that we must be completely subject to Him. John Newton suggested that there is yet another relation between these two things: not only is our taking of Christ's yoke upon us an indispensable requirement for our learning of Him, but also our learning of Him is His duly appointed means to enable us to wear His yoke.

"Learn of me." Be not afraid to come to Me for help and instruction, "for I am meek and lowly in heart." Here is encouragement. You need not hesitate to come to such a One, the Maker of heaven and earth, King of kings and

Lord of lords. He is the One before whom all the angels of heaven prostrate themselves in homage, yet the One who is the Friend of sinners. He is able to solve our every problem and supply strength for the weakest; because He is Man, possessed of human sensibilities, therefore is He capable of being "touched with the feeling of our infirmities."

"Learn of me." I know why these things appear so hard. It is owing to the pride and impatience of your hearts. To remedy this, take Me for your example; I require nothing of you but what I have performed before you, and on your account: in that path I mark out for you, you may perceive My own footsteps all the way. This is a powerful argument, a sweet recommendation, the yoke of Christ, to those who love Him, that He bore it Himself. He is not like the Pharisees, whom He censured (Matthew 23:4) on this very account: who bound heavy burdens, and grievous to be borne, and laid them on men's shoulders, but they themselves would not move them with one of their fingers.

1. Are you terrified with the difficulties attending your profession: disheartened by hard usage, or too ready to show resentment against those who oppose you? Learn of Jesus, admire and imitate His constancy: "Consider him who endured the contradiction of sinners against himself" (Heb. 12:3). Make a comparison (so the word imports) between yourself and Him, between the contradiction which He endured and that which you are called to struggle with; then surely you will be ashamed to complain. Admire and imitate His meekness: when He was reviled, He reviled not again; when He suffered, He threatened not; He wept for His enemies, and prayed for His murderers. Let the same mind be in you which was also in Christ Jesus.

2. Do you find it hard to walk steadfastly in His precepts, especially in some particular instances, when the maxims of worldly prudence and the pleadings of flesh and blood, are strongly against you? Learn of Jesus. He pleased not Himself (Rom. 15:3): He considered not what was safe and easy, but what was the will of His heavenly Father. Entreat Him to strengthen you with strength in your soul, that as you bear the name of His disciples, you may resemble Him in every part of your conduct, and shine as lights in a dark and selfish world, to the glory of His grace.

3. Are you tempted to repine at the dispensations of Divine providence? Take Jesus for your pattern. Did He say, when the unspeakable sufferings He was to endure for sinners were just coming upon Him, "The cup which my Father hath given me, shall I not drink it?" (John 18:11); and shall we

presume to have a will of our own? especially when we further reflect, that as His sufferings were wholly on our account, so all our sufferings are by His appointment, and all designed by Him to promote our best, that is our spiritual and eternal welfare? (John Newton).

"Learn of me." Christ, then, taught His disciples not only by precept, but also by example, not only by word of mouth but also by His own perfect life of obedience to the Father's will. When He uttered these words (Matthew 11:29) He was wearing the "yoke" and personally exemplifying meekness and lowliness. What a perfect Teacher, showing us in His own selflessness what these graces really are. He did not associate with the noble and mighty, but made fishermen His ambassadors and sought out the most despised, so that He was dubbed "a friend of publicans and sinners."

"And learn of me, for I am meek and lowly in heart." Those heavenly graces, the roots from which all other spiritual excellencies spring, can only be learned from Christ. The colleges and seminaries cannot impart them, preachers and churches cannot bestow them, no self-culture can attain unto them. They can only be learned experimentally at the feet of Christ, only as we take His yoke upon us. They can only be learned as we commune with Him and follow the example He left us. They can only be learned as we pray that we may be more fully conformed to His image and trustfully seek the enablement of His Spirit to "mortify the deeds of the body.

"What causes have we to mourn that there is so little meekness and lowliness in us! How we need to confess unto God our lamentable deficiency. Yet, merely mourning does not improve matters. We must go to the root of our folly and judge it. Why have I failed to learn these heavenly graces? Has it not to be said of me, as of Israel, "Ephraim is a bullock unaccustomed to the yoke?" Not until my proud spirit is broken and my will completely surrendered to Christ, can I truly "learn of Him."

And taking Christ's yoke upon us and learning of Him is a daily thing. Christianity is far more than a creed or ethical code—it is a being conformed practically to the image of God's Son. So many make the great mistake in supposing that coming to Christ and taking His yoke is a single act, which may be done once and for all. Not so! It is to be a continuous and daily act, "To whom coming [again and again], as unto a living stone" (1 Pet. 2:4). We need to continue as we began. The mature Christian who has been fifty years in the way needs Christ as urgently now as he did the first moment he was convicted of his lost condition. He needs to daily take His yoke and learn of

Him.

CHAPTER 19
The Leadership of Christ

"For My Yoke Is Easy and my burden is light" (Matthew 11:30). As pointed out (see chapter 43) the yoke, employed figuratively, is the symbol of service. Such an instrument united oxen together in pulling the plow or wagon, so they worked for their master. Our text refers to the service of Christ, in contrast to the service of sin and Satan. The devil promises his subjects a grand time if they follow his promptings, but sooner or later they discover, "the way of transgressors is hard" (Prov. 13:15). Sin deceives. Its deluded victims imagine they enjoy liberty while indulging the lusts of the flesh; but when failing health suggests they had better change their ways, they discover they are bound by habits they cannot break. Sin is a more cruel taskmaster than were the Egyptians to the Hebrews. And the service of Satan imposes far heavier burdens than Pharaoh ever placed upon his slaves. But "My yoke is easy, and my burden is light."

This declaration of the Savior may also be the sequel to His opening words in this passage. There He invited those who labored and were heavy laden, which may be understood in a twofold sense: those who were sick of sin and bowed down by a sense of its guilt, and those who labored to meet the requirements of divine holiness and are cast down by their inability to do so. Those who seek to fulfill the letter of God's Law, far from finding it "easy," discover it is very hard; while those who endeavor to work out a righteousness of their own to gain God's esteem, find it a heavy task and not a "light burden."

"For my yoke is easy, and my burden is light." Exactly what is the relation between this verse and the ones preceding? To which of the previous clauses is it more immediately connected? We cannot discover that any commentator has made any specific attempt to answer this question. We deem it wise to link these closing words of the Redeemer with each of the earlier utterances. Thus, "Come unto me, all ye that labor and are heavy laden, and I will give you rest; for my yoke is easy, and my burden is light. There is encouragement for us to come and proof that He will give us rest. "Take my yoke upon you": you need not fear to do so, "for my yoke is easy, and my burden is light." "And learn of me," for not only am I "meek and lowly in heart, and ye shall find rest unto your souls," but "for my yoke is easy."

"For my yoke is easy." The Greek word is variously rendered, "good," "kind," "gracious." There is nothing to chafe or hurt, rather is it pleasant to wear. The question has been raised if Christ spoke absolutely or relatively. That is, did He describe what the yoke was in itself, or how that yoke appeared to His people? We believe both senses are included. Assuredly Christ's yoke or service is a light or gracious one in itself, for all His commandments are framed by infinite wisdom and love and are designed for the good of those who receive them. So far from being a harsh tyrant who imposes hard duties for the mere sake of exerting His authority, Christ is a gracious Master who ever has in mind the welfare and highest interests of His subjects. His commandments "are not grievous" in themselves, but beneficent. The "father of lies" affirms Christ's yoke to be difficult and heavy.

But not only is the yoke of Christ "easy" in itself, but also it should be so in the sense and apprehension of His people. It will be so, if they do as He bids. The unregenerate find the yoke of Christ irksome and heavy, for it grates against the carnal nature. The service of Christ is drudgery to those in love with the world and who find their delight in fleshly lusts; but to one whose heart has been captivated by Christ, to be under His yoke is pleasant. If we come to Christ daily to be renewed by His grace, to yield ourselves afresh to His rule; if we sit at His feet to be taught of Him the loveliness of meekness and lowliness: if we enjoy spiritual communion with Him and partake of His rest, then whatsoever He commands is delightful to us, and we prove for ourselves that "wisdom's ways are ways of pleasantness, and all her paths are peace" (Prov. 3:17).

Here the Christian may discover the most conclusive evidence that a good work of grace has begun in his heart. How many poor souls are deeply distressed over this point. They ask themselves continually, Have I been genuinely converted or am I yet in a state of nature? They keep themselves in needless suspense because they fail to apply the scriptural methods of confirmation. Instead of measuring themselves by the rules in the Word, they await some extraordinary sensation in their heart. But many have been deceived at this point, for Satan can produce happy sensations in the heart and deep impressions on the mind. How much better is the testimony of an enlightened conscience. Judging things by the Word of God, it perceives that the yoke of Christ is easy and light.

But this principle works both ways. If we find by experience that Christ's yoke is easy and His burden is light then what must be said of a vast number of professing Christians who, by their own conduct, often avow that the Lord's service is burdensome? Though members of evangelical churches, may we conclude they are of the class who have a name that they live, and yet are dead (Rev. 3: 1)? Certainly we cannot allow that Christ made a false predication of His yoke. Then only one alternative is left. We are obliged to regard as strangers to godliness those who find a life of communion with the Lord and devotedness to His service dull or irksome.

Do not misunderstand this point. We are not affirming the Christian life is nothing but a bed of roses, or that when a person comes to Christ and takes His yoke that his troubles end. Not so. Instead, in a real sense his troubles only then begin. It is written, "Yea, and all that will live godly in Christ Jesus shall suffer persecution" (2 Tim. 3:12). Wearing the yoke of Christ unites us to Him; and union with Him brings us into "fellowship with His sufferings." The members of Christ's body, share the experience of their Head. The world hated and persecuted Him, and it hates those who bear His image. But the more closely we walk with Christ, the more we will suffer the hostility of Satan, for his rage is stirred up when he finds he has lost another of his captives.

Not only does the one who truly comes to Christ and takes upon him His yoke evoke the hatred of Satan and of the world, but also he is now the subject of inward conflicts. The corrupt nature which was his at birth is neither removed nor refined when he becomes a Christian. It remains within him, unchanged. But now he is more conscious of its presence and its vileness. Moreover, that evil nature opposes every movement of the holy nature he received at the new birth. "The flesh lusteth against the Spirit, and the Spirit against the flesh: and these are contrary the one to the other" (Gal. 5:17). This discovery of the plague of his own heart and that within there is opposition to holy aspirations, is a source of deep anguish to the child of God. He often cries, "O wretched man that I am! who shall deliver me from this body of death?" (Rom. 7:24).

We cannot affirm that the Christian's life is one of unclouded sunshine; yet we must not convey the impression the believer's lot is far from being envious, and that he is worse off than the unbeliever. Far from it. If the Christian uses diligently the means of God's appointing, he will possess a peace which passeth all understanding, and experience joys the worldling knows nothing about. The world may frown and the devil rage against him, but an approving conscience, the smile of God, the communion with fellow-believers, and the assurance of eternity with his Beloved, are ample compensation.

What is there in the yoke of Christ which makes such amends for the enmity it evokes and the suffering it entails, so that the believer will attest that it is an easy one? In seeking to answer this question we shall avail ourself of the help of John Newton's sermons, in outline. First, those who wear the yoke of Christ act from a principle which makes all things easy. This is love. Any yoke will chafe when resisted, but even one of cast-iron would be pleasant if it were lined with felt and padded with wool. And this is what renders the yoke of Christ easy to His people. It is lined with love, His to them, and theirs to Him. Whenever the shoulder becomes sore, look to the lining! Keep the lining right and the yoke will be no more a burden to us than wings are to a bird, or a wedding ring to a bride.

Scripture records that when Jacob served a hard master seven years for Rachel, they seemed but a few days to him "for the love he had to her" (Gen. 29:20). What a difference it makes when we perform a difficult task, whether for a stranger or a dear friend, an exacting employer or a close relative. Affection makes the hardest joy easy. But there is no love like that which a redeemed sinner bears to Him who died in his stead. We are willing to suffer much to gain the affection of one we highly esteem, even though we are not sure of success; but when we know the affection is reciprocal, it gives added strength for the endeavor. The believer does not love with uncertainty. He knows that Christ loved him before he had any love for the Savior; yes, loved him even when his own heart was filled with enmity against Him. This love supplies two sweet and effectual motives in service: A desire to please. This is the question love is ever asking. What can I do to gratify, to make happy the object of my affection? Love is ever ready to do whatever it can, and regrets that it cannot do more. Neither time, difficulties, nor expense concern the one whose heart is warmly engaged. But the world is not in the secret. They neither know nor appreciate the principles which motivate the people of God. Not only are they at a loss to understand why the Christian is no longer willing to join with them in the pleasures of sin, but also they fail to see what satisfaction he finds in reading the Scriptures, in secret prayer, or public worship. They suppose that some mental derangement is responsible, and advise him to leave such gloomy exercises to those on the verge of the grave. But the believer can answer, "the love of Christ constraineth me."

A pleasant assurance of acceptance. What a difference it makes when we are able to determine whether or not what we do will be favorably received. If we have reason to fear that the one for whom we work does not appreciate our efforts, we find little delight in the task and are tempted to spare ourselves. But if we have good reason to believe that our labors will meet with a smile of approval, how much easier is the labor and how much more readily will we do it with our might. It is this encouragement which stimulates Christ's disciples. They know that He will not overlook the smallest service in His name or the slightest suffering endured for His sake; for even a cup of cold water given on His account is acknowledged as though proffered immediately to Him (Mark 9:41).

Second, service is still easier and lighter if it is agreeable to our inclinations. Esau would probably have done anything to please his father to obtain the blessing. But no commandment could have been more agreeable to him than to be sent for venison, because he was a hunter (Gen. 25:27). The Christian has received from God a new nature, he has been made "a partaker of the divine nature" (2 Pet. 1:4). Just as the magnetic needle ever points to the North Star, so this spiritual principle ever turns to its Author. Consequently, God's Word is its food, communion with Him its desire, His Law its delight. True, he still groans under inward corruption, but these are part of sin's burden and no part of Christ's yoke. He groans because he cannot serve Him better. But just so far as he exercises his faith he rejoices in every part of Christ's yoke. Professing His name is a holy privilege, His precepts are a profitable meditation, and suffering for Christ's sake is counted an high honor.

Third, the burden of Christ is light because sustaining grace is granted to its wearer. Service to a loved one would be impracticable if you were infirm and incapacitated. Nor could you take a long journey to minister to a friend, no matter how dear, if you were crippled. But the yoke of Christ is easy in this respect too—He supplies sufficient strength to the bearer. What is hard to flesh and blood is easy to faith and grace. It is true, apart from Christ the believer "can do nothing" (John 15:5); but it is equally true he "can do all things" through Christ strengthening him (Phil. 4:13). It is true that, "Even the youths shall faint and be weary, and the young men shall utterly fall"; yet we are divinely assured "they that wait upon the LORD shall renew their strength; they shall mount up with wings as eagles; they shall run, and not be weary; they shall walk, and not faint" (Isa. 40:30-31). What more can we ask? It is entirely our own fault if we are not "strong in the Lord, and in the power of his might" (Eph. 6:10).

Whatever the Lord may call upon us to do, if we depend on Him in the use of appointed means, He will most certainly equip us for it. He is no Pharaoh, requiring us to make bricks and providing no straw for the same. So far from it, He promises, "as thy days, so shall thy strength be" (Deut. 33:25). Moses may complain, "I am slow of speech, and of a slow tongue," but the Lord assures him," I will be with thy mouth, and teach thee what thou shalt say" (Ex. 4:10, 12). Paul acknowledged, "Not that we are sufficient of ourselves to think any thing as of ourselves;" yet he at once added, "but our sufficiency is of God" (2 Cor. 3:5). So too whatever sufferings the Lord calls upon His people to endure for His sake, He will assuredly grant sustaining grace. "All power in heaven and in earth" belongs unto Christ and therefore is He able to make our enemies flee before us and deliver from the mouth of the lion. Even though He permits His servants to be beaten and cast into prison, yet songs of praises are put into their mouths (Acts 16:25).

Finally, the easiness of Christ's yoke appears in the rich compensations that accompany it. Under sin's yoke we spent our strength for what did not satisfy, but when wearing Christ's yoke we find rest for our souls. If we live a life of pleasing self and seeking our own honor, then we reap misery and woe; but when self is denied and Christ is glorified, peace and joy is ours. No man serves Christ for nothing: in keeping His commandments there is "great reward" (Ps. 19:11)—not of debt, but of grace, after. The Christian may have much to cast him down, but he has far more to cheer him up and send him on his way rejoicing. He has free access to the throne of grace, precious promises to rest upon, and the consolation of the Holy Spirit to comfort his soul. He has a Friend who sticketh closer than a brother, a loving Father who supplies his every need, and the blessed assurance that when the appointed hour arrives he shall go to another world, where there is no sin or sorrow, but "fullness of joy," and "pleasures for evermore" (Ps. 16:11).

CHAPTER 20
The Example of Christ

Two serious mistakes have been made by men in taking or not taking Christ for their example. It is difficult to determine which is the more evil and fatal of the two. First, those who held up the perfect life of the Lord Jesus before the uncoverted maintained that they must imitate it in order to find acceptance with God. In other words, they made emulating Christ "the way of salvation" to lost sinners. This is a fundamental error, which cannot be resisted too strenuously. It repudiates the total depravity and spiritual helplessness of fallen man. It denies the necessity for the new birth. It nullifies the atonement by emphasizing Christ's flawless life at the expense of His sacrificial death. It substitutes works for faith, creature efforts for divine grace, man's faulty doings for the Redeemer's finished work. If the Acts and epistles are searched it will be revealed that the apostles never preached imitating Christ as the way to obtain forgiveness of sins and secure peace with God.

But in recent generations the pendulum has swung to the opposite extreme. If, a century ago, the example which Christ has left His people was made too much of, our moderns make far too little of it; if they gave it a place in preaching to the unsaved which Scripture does not warrant, we have failed to press it upon Christians to the extent Scripture requires. If those a century ago are to be blamed for misusing the example of Christ in connection with justification, we are guilty of failing to use it in connection with sanctification. While it is true that the moral perfections which Christ displayed during His earthly sojourn are still extolled in many places, how rarely one hears (or reads) of those who insist that emulating Christ is absolutely essential for the believer's preservation and ultimate salvation. Would not the great majority of orthodox preachers be positively afraid to make any such assertion, lest they be charged with legality?

The Lord Jesus Christ is not only a perfect and glorious Pattern of all graces, holiness, virtue, and obedience, to be preferred above all others, but also He alone is such. In the lives of the best of the saints, Scripture records what it is our duty to avoid, as well as what we ought to follow. Sometimes one is puzzled to know whether it is safe to conform to them or not. But God has graciously supplied us with a sure rule which solves that problem. If we heed it we will never be at a loss to see our duty. Holy men and women of Scripture are to be imitated by us only as far as they were themselves conformed unto Christ (1 Cor. 11:1). The best of their graces, the highest of their attainments, the most perfect of their duties, were spoiled by blemishes; but in Christ there is no imperfection whatever, for He had no sin and did no sin.

Christ is not only the perfect, but also the pattern Man; and therefore is His example suitable for all believers. This remarkable fact presents a feature which has not received the attention it deserves. There is nothing so distinctive in personality as racial and national characteristics. The greatest of men bear unmistakable marks of their heredity and environment. Racial peculiarities are imperishable; to the last fiber of his being, Luther was a German, Knox a Scot; and with all his largeness of heart, Paul was a Jew. In sharp contrast, Jesus Christ rose above heredity and environment. Nothing local, transient, national, or sectarian dwarfed His wondrous personality. Christ is the only truly catholic man. He belongs to all ages and is related to all men, because He is "the Son of man." This underlies the universal suitability of Christ's example to believers of all nations, who one and all may find in Him the perfect realization of their ideal.

This is indeed a miracle, and exhibits a transcendent perfection in the Man Christ Jesus which is rarely pondered. How remarkable that the converted Englishman may find in Christ's character and conduct a pattern as well-suited to him as to a saved Chinese; that His example is as appropriate for the regenerated Zulu as for a born-again German. The needs of Lord Bacon and Sir Isaac Newton were as truly met in Christ as were those of the half-witted youth who said, "I'm a poor sinner and nothing at all, But Jesus Christ is my all in all." How remarkable that the example of Christ is as appropriate for believers of the twentieth century as it was for those of the first, that it is as suitable for a Christian child as for his grandparent!

He is appointed of God for this very purpose. One end why God sent His Son to become flesh and tabernacle in the world was that He might set before us an example in our nature, in One who was like unto us in all things, sin excepted. Thereby He exhibited to us that renewal to His image in us, of that return to Him from sin and apostasy, and of that holy obedience He requires of us. Such an example was needful so that we might never be at a loss about the will of God in His commandments, having a glorious representation of it before our eyes. That could be given us no other way than in our own nature. The nature of angels was not suited as an example of obedience, especially in the exercise of such graces as we specially stand in need of in this world. What example could angels set us in patience in afflictions or quietness in sufferings, when their nature is incapable of such things? Nor could we have had a perfect example in our nature except in one who was holy and "separate from sinners."

Many Scriptures present Christ as the believer's Exemplar: "Take my yoke upon you and learn of me; for I am meek and lowly in heart" (Matthew 11:29),—learn by the course of My life as well as by My words; "When he putteth forth his own sheep, he goeth before them, and the sheep follow him" (John 10:4)—He requires no more of us than He rendered Himself; "I have given you an example, that ye should do as I have done to you" (John 13:15); "Now the God of patience and consolation grant you to be likeminded one toward another according to Christ Jesus" (Rom. 15:5); "Let this mind be in you, which was also in Christ Jesus" (Phil. 2:5). "Let us run with patience the race that is set before us, looking unto Jesus, the author and finisher of our faith" (Heb. 12:1-2); "But if, when ye do well, and suffer for it, ye take it patiently, this is acceptable unto God. For even hereunto were ye called: because Christ also suffered for us, leaving us an example, that ye should follow his steps" (1 Pet. 2:20-21); "He that saith he abideth in him ought himself so to walk, even as he walked" (1 John 2:6).

Example is better than precept. Why? Because a precept is more or less an abstraction, whereas an example sets before us a concrete representation; therefore has more aptitude to incite the mind to imitation. The conduct of those with whom we are in close association exerts a considerable influence upon us, either for good or evil. The fact is clearly recognized in the Scriptures. For example, we are enjoined, "Make no friendship with an angry man; and with a furious man thou shalt not go: lest thou learn his ways, and get a snare to thy soul" (Prov. 22:24-25). It was for this reason that God commanded the Israelites to utterly destroy all the inhabitants of Canaan, so that they might not learn their evil ways and be contaminated by them (Deut. 7:2-4). Contrariwise, the example of the pious exerts an influence for good; that is why they are called "the salt of the earth."

In keeping with this principle, God has appointed the consideration of Christ's character and conduct as a special means to increase the piety in His people. As their hearts contemplate His holy obedience, it has a peculiar efficacy to their growing in grace beyond all other examples. It is in beholding the Lord Jesus by faith that salvation comes to us. "Look unto me, and be ye saved, all the ends of the earth" (Isa. 45:22). Christ is presented before the sinner in the Gospel, with the promise that whosoever believingly looks to Him shall not perish, but have everlasting life (John 3:14-15). This is a special ordinance of God, and it is made effectual by the Spirit to all who believe. In like manner, Christ is presented to the saints as the grand Pattern of obedience and Example of holiness, with the promise that as they contemplate Him as such we shall be changed into His image (2 Cor. 3:18). Our response to that appointment of God is rewarded by a growing in piety.

But to get down to details: what is involved in the saints' imitating of Christ? First, it presupposes that they be already regenerate. The hearts of His followers must be sanctified before their lives can be conformed to Him. The spirit and principle of obedience must be imparted to the soul before there can be an external imitation of Christ's practice. This order is plainly enunciated in, "I will give them one heart, and I will put a new spirit within you; and I will take the stony heart out of their flesh, and will give them a heart of flesh: that they may walk in my statutes, and keep mine ordinances, and do them: and they shall be my people, and I will be their God" (Ezek. 11:19-20). One who is yet in the gall of bitterness and the bond of iniquity has no heart for spiritual things; therefore the tree must be made good before it can produce good fruit. We must first live in the Spirit and then walk in the Spirit (Gal. 5:25). One might as well urge the Ethiopian to change his skin or the leopard his spots, as call upon the unconverted to follow the example Christ has left His people.

Second, imitating Christ definitely denotes that no Christian may govern himself or act according to his own will. Those who are a rule to themselves act in fearful defiance of the Most High. "O LORD, I know that the way of man is not in himself: it is not in man that walketh to direct his steps" (Jer. 10:23). A man may as well feign to be his own creator as his own guide. No man has wisdom enough to direct himself. When born again we are conscious of this fact. Our proud hearts are humbled and our rebellious wills broken, and we feel the need of being led by Another. The cry of a converted heart is, "Lord, what wouldst thou have me to do?" His answer to us today is,

117

follow the example which I have left you, learn of me, walk as I walked.

Third, if this imitating of Christ clearly implies that no man may pretend to be his own master, it is equally evident that no matter how wise or how holy he is, no Christian has the right or is qualified to rule others. Christ alone is appointed and fitted to be the Lord of His people. It is true that we read in the Word, "That ye be not slothful, but followers of them who through faith and patience inherit the promises" (Heb. 6:12); and "Obey them that have the rule over you, and submit yourselves: for they watch for your souls, as they that must give account" (Heb. 13:17). Yet that must be taken in subordination to the example of Christ. The best of men are but men at the best; they have their errors and faults, and where they differ from Christ it is our duty to differ from them. It is very important that we be quite clear upon this point, for much mischief has resulted from allowing some to deprive others of a vital part of their rightful liberty.

It is not that Scripture teaches an ecclesiastical democracy, that is as far from the truth as the Romish hierarchy at the opposite extreme. God has placed rulers in the Church, and its members are commanded to obey them; but their rule is administrative and not legislative—to enforce the laws of Christ, and not invent rules of their own. Paul affirmed, "Not for that we have dominion over your faith, but are helpers of your joy: for by faith ye stand" (2 Cor. 1:24); and Peter declared of the elders or bishops, "Neither as being lords over God's heritage, but being ensamples to the flock" (1 Pet. 5:3). Filled with so great a measure of the Spirit of wisdom and holiness as Paul was, yet he goes no higher than this; "Be ye followers of me, even as I also am of Christ" (1 Cor. 11:1).

Fourth, the imitation of Christ plainly intimates that true Christianity is very strict and exacting, and in no wise countenances licentiousness or the indulgence of fleshly lusts. This needs emphases in such a day as ours, when so much laxity prevails. People suppose they may be followers of Christ and yet ignore the path which He traveled; that they may decline the unpleasant task of denying self and yet make sure of heaven. What a delusion! The vital necessity of the careful imitation of Christ disallows all loose walking, and rejects the claim of any to being real Christians if they do not heed His example. Neither worldliness nor self-indulgence can find any protection beneath the wings of the Gospel. The unvarying rule, binding on all who claim to be His, is "Let every one that nameth the name of Christ depart from iniquity" (2 Tim. 2:19). Let him either follow the example of Christ, or cease claiming to belong to Him; let him tread the highway of holiness or all his fair words are worthless.

Fifth, the imitation of Christ necessarily implies the blemishes of the best of men. If the life of Christ is our pattern, then the holiest among His followers are obliged to admit they come far short of this standard of duty, and not in a few details, but in every respect. The character and conduct of the Lord Jesus were without spot or blemish; therefore they are so high above our poor attainments that we are filled with shame when we measure ourselves by them. Self-satisfied religionists may take delight in comparing themselves with others, as the Pharisee did with the publican. Deluded souls who suppose that all Christian holiness consists of is measuring up to some humanly invented standard of perfection (or entering into some peculiar experience), may pride themselves that they have "received the second blessing," or "have the fullness or baptism of the Spirit;" yet all who honestly measure themselves by the perfections of Christ will find abundant cause to be humbled.

This too, is a point of tremendous practical importance. If I place my handkerchief against a dark background, it will appear spotlessly clean; but, if I lay it upon newly fallen snow, the imperfection of its whiteness is quickly apparent. If I compare my own life with that preached by certain "victorious-life" advocates I may conclude that my life is quite acceptable. But if I diligently apply to myself the plumbline of Christ's example, then I must at once acknowledge, like Peter of old, I am but following Him "afar off." Surely none was more proficient in holiness and punctilious in obedience than Paul; yet, when he compared himself to Christ, he declared, "Not as though I had already attained, either were already perfect: but I follow after, if that I may apprehend" (Phil. 3:12).

Sixth, the imitation of Christ as our pattern clearly implies His transcendent holiness, that His holiness is high above that of all creatures. Therefore it is the greatest of the Christian's ambitions to be conformed to His image (Phil. 3:10). Christ has a double perfection: a perfection of being and a perfection of working. His life on earth supplies a perfect rule for us because there was no blot or error therein. He was "holy, harmless, undefiled, separate from sinners," and such an High Priest became us (Heb. 7:26). Thus the conformity of professing Christians to Christ's example is both the test and measure of all their graces. The nearer anyone approaches to this Pattern, the closer he comes to perfection.

Finally, the Christian's imitation of Christ, under the penalty of forfeiting his claim to any saving interest in Christ, necessarily denotes that sanctification and obedience are the evidences of our justification and acceptance with God. Scriptural assurance is unattainable without sincere and strict obedience. "The work of righteousness [not of loose living] shall be peace" (Isa. 32:17). "We have it not for our holiness, but we always have it in the way of holiness. Let men talk what they will of the immediate sealings and comforts of the Spirit, without any regard to holiness, or respect to obedience: sure I am, whatever delusion they meet with in that way, true peace and consolation is only to be found and expected here" (John Flavel, to whom we are indebted for much in the seven points).

"Christ also suffered for us, leaving us an example, that ye should follow his steps" (1 Pet. 2:21). We have seen that not only is the perfect life of Christ a suitable pattern of holiness and obedience for His people to imitate, but also that God has expressly appointed it for that purpose. This is so that we may have a sure rule to walk by, the Law of God translated into concrete terms and its requirements set before us by a personal representation; and also for the purpose of humbling our proud hearts, by revealing to us how far short we come of measuring up to God's standard of righteousness. Furthermore, God has appointed that the example of Christ should be followed by His people so that His Son might be honored by them; to distinguish His followers from the world; and so that they should evidence the reality of their profession. Imitating Christ, then, is not optional, but obligatory.

But here a very real difficulty confronts those who sincerely seek grace to heed this divine appointment. In what particular respects are we to regard Christ as our Exemplar? All things recorded of Him in Holy Writ are for our instruction, but not all for our imitation. There were some things Christ did as God; for example, He wrought miracles. "My Father worketh hitherto, and I work . . . For as the Father raiseth up the dead, and quickeneth them; even so the Son quickeneth whom he will" (John 5:17, 21); "But that ye may know that the Son of man hath power on earth to forgive sins, (then saith he to the sick of and palsy), Arise, take up thy bed, and go unto thine house" (Matthew 9:6)—even the apostles never performed such deeds in their own name or by their own power. Again; as Mediator, He performed works of merit, thus making expiation for the sins of His people and "bringing in everlasting righteousness" for them, and obtaining their justification and reconciliation. So now His intercession secures their preservation. No mere man can do anything meritorious, for at best we are all "unprofitable servants."

Even as Man, Christ performed extraordinary acts which are not for our emulation: fasting for forty days and nights, walking on the water, spending a whole night in prayer (Luke 6:12)—we do not read in Scripture of anyone else doing so—are cases in point. So He performed certain temporary works which pertained to the time in which He lived, which are not for our imitation—such as His being circumcised, keeping the Passover. Wherein, then, is Christ to be imitated by us? First, in all those moral duties which pertain to all men at all times, which are neither extraordinary nor temporary, comprehended in the loving of God with all our hearts and our neighbors as ourselves. Second, in such duties as belong to a like calling: as the child obeying its parents (Luke 2:51); the citizen paying his taxes (Matthew 17:27); the minister of the Gospel diligently (Luke 8:1) and faithfully (Heb. 3:2) discharging his office. Third, in all such works as have like reason and occasion for doing them (Matthew 12:12; John 8:59).

The believer's conformity to Christ corresponds to the states through which He passed. Christ Jesus first entered a state of humiliation, before God rewarded Him by bringing Him into a state of exaltation. Therefore has God ordered that the members shall resemble their Head. They are called upon to endure sufferings, before they enter into the promised glory. The disciples of the Lord Jesus have to experience a measure of opposition, persecution, hatred, affliction, and they do so for their hope of a better life to come. In that, they do but follow "the captain of their salvation," who was "made perfect through sufferings" (Heb. 2:10). Has not God declared, "If we be dead with him [Christ], we shall also live with him: if we suffer, we shall also reign with him" (2 Tim. 2:11-12). That order is inescapable, "Always bearing about in the body the dying of the Lord Jesus, that the life also of Jesus might be made manifest in our body" (2 Cor. 4:10).

In like manner, the Christian is to be conformed to the special acts of Christ's mediation, which are His death and resurrection. These are of paramount consideration, for they are not only a pattern proposed to our meditation, but also a great influence upon our dying to sin and living unto holiness. This is evidenced from the fact that those effects of grace in us are ascribed to those acts of Christ's mediation which carry most correspondence with them. Thus our mortification is ascribed to Christ's crucifixion (Gal.

2:20); our vivification to His rising unto life (Phil. 3:10); and our heavenly mindedness to His ascension (Phil. 3:20); so that all of those chief acts of Christ are verified in His people. We die to sin as Christ died for it.

But in descending to more specific details, it is in Christ's graces we are to be conformed to Him. All the graces and virtues of the Spirit were represented in their grandest glory and brightest luster in His life here on earth. First, the purity and holiness of His life is proposed as a glorious pattern for the saints to imitate. "Every man that hath this hope in him purifieth himself, even as he is pure" (1 John 3:3). Before enlarging upon this, let us point out where Christ is unique and beyond our imitation. He was essentially holy in His being, for He is "the Holy One of God." He entered this world immaculate, pure from the least stain of pollution, "That holy thing which shall be born of thee" (Luke 1:35). Again, He was effectually holy, for He makes others holy. By His sufferings and blood there opened a fountain "for sin and for uncleanness" (Zech. 13:1). He is also infinitely holy, as He is God, and no measure can be set upon His holiness as Mediator, for He received the Spirit without measure (John 3:34). In these particulars He is inimitable.

Notwithstanding these exceptions, the holiness of Christ is a pattern for us. He was truly and sincerely holy, without fiction or pretense. When the prince of this world scrutinized Him he could find no defect in Him (John 14:30). He was pure gold throughout. The Pharisee may pretend to be holy, but it is only in outward appearance. Now the Christian's holiness must be genuine, sincere, without simulation. Christ was uniformly holy, at one time and place as well as another. The same even tenor of holiness ran through the whole of His life from first to last. So should it be with His followers. "As he which hath called you is holy, so be ye holy in all manner of conversation" (1 Pet. 1:15). What inconsistencies we have to bemoan; one part of our life heavenly, another earthly.

Christ was exemplarily holy; a pattern to all that came near Him, so that even those sent to arrest Him had to return to their masters and say, "never man spake as this man." We are to imitate Him in this respect. The Thessalonian saints were commended because they, "were ensamples to all that believe in Macedonia and Achaia. For from you sounded out the word of the Lord not only in Macedonia and Achaia, but also in every place your faith to God-ward is spread abroad" (1 Thess. 1:7-8). Let none go out of our company without being either convicted or edified. Christ was strictly holy.

"Which of you convicteth me of sin?" was His challenge. The most observing and unfriendly eye could pick no flaw in His actions. It is our duty to imitate Christ in this too, "That ye may be blameless and harmless, the sons of God, without rebuke, in the midst of a crooked and perverse nation, among whom ye shine as lights in the world" (Phil. 2:15).

Second, the obedience of Christ to His Father's will is a pattern for the Christian's emulation. "Let this mind be in you, which was also in Christ Jesus . . . [who] became obedient unto death" (Phil. 2:5, 8). Christ's obedience was free and voluntary, not forced and compulsory. "Then said I, Lo, I come . . . I delight to do thy will, O my God" (Ps. 40:7-8). Nor did He waver, later, when suffering so grievously in the discharge of that will. "Therefore doth my Father love me, because I lay down my life" (John 10:17). So the Christian is to follow the steps of Christ, doing nothing grudgingly and counting not God's commands grievous. Our obedience must be rendered cheerfully if it is to be acceptable. See His perfect submission in Gethsemane. Here too He left us an example. We are to make no demur to the most unpleasant task God assigns us. Happy the Christian who can say with the apostle, "for I am ready not to be bound only, but also to die at Jerusalem for the name of the Lord Jesus" (Acts 21:13).

The obedience of Christ was entirely disinterested. It was wrought for no self ends, but for the glory of God. "I have glorified thee on the earth. I have finished the work which thou gavest me to do" (John 17:4). Christ sought not honor of men, but the great desire of His soul was "Father, glorify Thy name" (John 12:28). This quality must also characterize our obedience. "Look not every man on his own things, but every man also on the things of others" (Phil. 2:4). The streams of Christ's obedience flowed from the fountain of love to God. "But that the world may know that I love the Father, and as the Father gave me commandment, even so I do" (John 14:13). Let this also be true of us, for loveless obedience is of no value in the sight of God. The obedience of Christ was constant, continuing to His very last breath. Being not "weary in well-doing" is required of us. "Be thou faithful unto death" (Rev. 2:10).

Third, the self-denial of Christ is the pattern for the believer. "If any man wilt come after me, let him deny himself, and take up his cross, and follow me" (Matthew 16:24). Though there is to be a resemblance, there can be no exact equivalent. "For ye know the grace of our Lord Jesus Christ, that, though he was rich, yet for your sakes he became poor" (2 Cor. 8:9). Who can gauge what Christ, for the glory of God and the love which He bare to the elect, gave up for us? How trivial in comparison is the greatest sacrifice we are called upon to make! Christ was under no obligation whatever to deny Himself for us, but He has placed us under the strongest obligation to deny ourselves for His sake. Though under no obligation, He denied Himself readily, making no objection to the severest part of it. Then let it not be said of us, "For all seek their own, not the things which are Jesus Christ's" (Phil. 2:21). Let not self be loved, petted, pitied, pampered, and indulged; rather renounce and mortify it, and make pleasing and glorifying Christ your great business.

Fourth, the activity and diligence of Christ in fulfilling the work of God committed unto Him, was a pattern for all believers to imitate. It is said of Him that He "went about doing good" (Acts 10:38). What a glorious work He accomplished in so short a time!—a work which will be celebrated through all eternity by the praises of the redeemed, a work upon which His heart was intently set. "My meat is to do the will of him that sent me" (John 4:34). It was a work under which He never fainted, despite the greatest opposition. The shortness of the time provoked Him to the greatest diligence. "I must work the works of him that sent me, while it is day: the night cometh, when no man can work" (John 9:4). He improved all opportunities and occasions: granting Nicodemus an interview at night, preaching the Gospel to the woman at the well when He was exhausted from His journey. Nothing displeased Him more than to be dissuaded from His work. "Get thee behind me, Satan," He said to Peter when the apostle said, "spare thyself, Lord."

Shall His followers trifle their lives away in vanity? Shall we be slothful when He was so diligent? How great an honor God has placed on us by calling us to His service. Steadfastness in the work of obedience is our greatest security in the hour of temptation. "The LORD is with you, while ye be with him" (2 Chron. 15:2). Diligence in prosecuting holiness is the way to get more (Luke 8:18). Graces grow by being used; spiritual acts lead to spiritual habits; talents faithfully employed are rewarded by an increase. Diligence in the work of God is the direct way to an assurance of the love of God (2 Pet. 1:5-10). Diligence in obedience is the greatest security against backsliding. Coldness leads to carelessness, carelessness to negligence, negligence to apostasy. The more diligent we are in serving God, the more our likeness to Christ.

Fifth, the inoffensiveness of the life of Christ on earth is an excellent pattern to all His people. He injured none, and never gave occasion for any to be justly injured by Him. He was not only holy, but also "harmless." He waived His own personal rights to avoid giving an offense, as in the case of tribute money. When he was reviled, He "reviled not again" (1 Pet. 2:23). So circumspect was our Savior that when His enemies sought occasion against Him, they could not find any (John 19:4). Let us earnestly seek grace that we may imitate this blessed excellency of His life, that we may obey God's command and be "blameless and harmless, the sons of God, without rebuke" (Phil. 2:15). The honor of Christ, whose name we bear, is bound up in our deportment. The rule which He has laid upon us, is "Be ye wise as serpents, and harmless as doves" Matthew 10:16).

Sixth, the humility and meekness of Christ is proposed by Himself as a pattern for His people's imitation. "Learn of me: for I am meek and lowly in heart" (Matthew 11:29). He abased Himself, by taking upon Him the form of a servant. He stooped to the lowest office by washing the disciples' feet. When He presented Himself to Israel as their King, it was in humiliation, riding upon the back of an ass. "Behold, thy King cometh unto thee, meek" (Matthew 21:5). He declared, "the Son of man came not to be ministered unto, but to minister" (Matthew 20:28). He condescended to the lowest of men, eating with "publicans and sinners" (Matthew 9:11). In all of this He left us an example to follow. O to be "clothed with humility" (1 Pet. 5:5), and thereby evidence our conformity to Christ.

Pride ill becomes one who professes to be a follower of the Lord Jesus. It not only betrays lack of communion with Christ, but also a woeful ignorance of self. Nothing is so provoking to God, and more quickly estranges the soul from Him. "Though the LORD is high, yet hath he respect unto the lowly; but the proud he knoweth afar off" (Ps. 138:6). Pride is totally inconsistent with the complaints we make of our corruptions, and it presents a serious stumbling block to the children of God. Be not ambitious of the world's great ones, but content yourself as one of Christ's little ones. Learn humility at His feet. Evidence it in your apparel and deportment (1 Pet. 3:3). Display it in cultivating fellowship with the poorest of the flock (Rom. 12:16). Show it by speaking of and comporting yourself as "less than the least of all saints" (Eph. 3:8).

Seventh, the contentment of Christ in a low and mean condition in this world is an excellent pattern for His people's imitation. His portion here was a condition of deepest poverty and contempt. The child of lowly parents; born in a manger. So deprived of the comforts of this world that, much of His time, He had not where to lay His head; so poor He had to borrow a penny to point out its superscription. Yet He never murmured or complained. Nay, so far from it, so perfectly content was He with God's appointments, that He declared, "The lines are fallen unto me in pleasant places" (Ps. 16:6). Under the most degrading sufferings, He never resisted: "He was oppressed, and he was afflicted, yet he opened not his mouth: he is brought as a lamb to the slaughter" (Isa. 53:7).

O that in this also the poorest Christians would imitate their Savior, and learn to manage an afflicted condition with a contented spirit: let there be no complaints, or foolish charging of God heard from you, whatever straits or troubles He brings you into.

The meanest and most afflicted Christian is owner of many rich, invaluable mercies (Eph. 1:3; 1 Corinthians 3:23). Is sin pardoned and God reconciled? then never open your mouths any more. You have many precious promises that God will not forsake you in your straits (Heb. 13:5). Your whole life has been an experience of the faithfulness of God to His promises. How useful and beneficial all your afflictions are to you! they purge your sins, wean you from the world, and turn to your salvation; then, how unreasonable must your discontentedness at them be! The time of your relief and full deliverance from all your troubles is at hand: the time is but short that you shall have any concernment about such things. Your lot falls by Divine direction upon you, and bad as it may be, it is much easier and sweeter than the condition of Christ in this world was. Yet He contented, and why not you? (John Flavel).

"He that saith he abideth in him ought himself also so to walk, even as he walked" (1 John 2:6). The principal design of the apostle in this epistle is to exhibit certain signs and marks, both negative and positive, for the examination or trial of men's claims to being Christians (1 John 5:13). It is in that light our verse must be interpreted. The proof of a saving interest in Christ is our imitation of Him. Were this criterion faithfully insisted upon today from the pulpit much of the empty profession now abounding would be clearly exposed. A claim is made, "He that saith he abideth in Him," which signifies an interest in and communion with Him. The only way that claim can be established is by walking as Christ walked, following the example He has left us.

Every man is bound to the imitation of Christ under penalty of forfeiting his claim to Christ. The necessity of this imitation of Christ convincingly appears divers ways. First, from the established order of salvation, which is fixed and unalterable. God that hath appointed the end, hath also established the means and order by which men shall attain the ultimate end. Now conformity to Christ is the established method in which God will bring many souls to glory. "For whom he did foreknow, he also did predestinate to be conformed to the image of his Son, that he might be the firstborn among many brethren" (Rom. 8:29). The same God who has predestinated men to salvation, has, in order, predestinated them to conformity to Christ. This order of heaven is never to be reversed; we may as well hope to be saved without Christ, as to be saved without conformity to Christ.

Secondly, the nature of Christ-mystical requires this conformity, and renders it indispensably necessary. Otherwise, the body of Christ must be heterogeneous: of a nature different from the Head, and how monstrous and uncomely would this be! This would represent Christ to the world in an image, or idea, much like that, "The head of fine gold, the breasts and arms of silver, the thighs of brass, the legs of iron, the feet part of iron and part of clay" (Dan. 2:32-33). Christ, the Head, is pure and holy, and therefore very unsuitable to sensual and worldly members. And therefore the apostle in his description of Christ-mystical, describes the members of Christ (as they ought to be) of the same nature and quality with the Head: "As is the heavenly, such are they also that are heavenly; and as we have borne the image of the earthy, so we shall also bear the image of the heavenly." That image or resemblance of Christ, which shall be complete and perfect after the resurrection, must be begun in its first draught here by the work of regeneration.

Thirdly, this resemblance and conformity to Christ appears necessary from the communion which all believers have with Him in the same spirit of grace and holiness. Believers are called Christ's "fellows" or co-partners (Ps. 45:7) from their participation with Him of the same Spirit. God giveth the same Spirit unto us, which He more plentifully poured out upon Christ. Now where the same Spirit and principle is, there the same fruits and operations must be produced, according to the proportions and measures of the Spirit of grace communicated; and this reason is farther enforced by the very design and end of God in the infusion of the Spirit of grace: for it is plain from Ezekiel 36:27 that practical holiness and obedience is the scope and design of that infusion of the Spirit. The very innate property of the Spirit of God in men is to elevate their minds, set their affections upon heavenly things, purge their hearts from earthly dross, and fit them for a life of holiness and obedience. Its nature also is assimilating and changeth them in whom it is into the same image with Jesus Christ, their Heavenly Head (2 Cor. 3:18).

Fourth, the necessity of this imitation of Christ may be argued from the design and end of Christ's exhibition to the world in a body of flesh. For though we detest that doctrine of the Socinians. which makes the exemplary life of Christ to be the whole end of His incarnation, yet we must not run so far from an error as to lose a precious truth. We say, the satisfaction of His blood was a main and principal end of His incarnation, according to Matthew 20:28. We affirm also, that it was a great design and end of the incarnation of Christ to set before us a pattern of holiness for our imitation, for so speaks the apostle: He "hath left us an example, that we should follow His steps" (1 Pet. 2:21); and this example of Christ greatly obliges believers to His imitation: "Let this mind be in you, which was also in Christ Jesus" (Phil. 2:5).

Fifthly, our imitation of Christ is one of those great articles which every man is to subscribe, whom Christ will admit into the number of His disciples. "Whosoever doth not bear his cross, and come after me, cannot be my disciple" (Luke 14:27): and again "If any man serve me, let him follow me" (John 12:26). To this condition we have submitted, if we be sincere believers; and therefore are strictly bound to the imitation of Christ, not only by God's command, but by our own consent. But if we profess interest in Christ, when our hearts never consented to follow, and imitate His example, then are we self-deceiving hypocrites, wholly disagreeing from the Scripture character of believers. They that are Christ's are there described as walking not after the flesh, but after the Spirit.

Sixthly, the honor of Christ necessitates the conformity of Christians to His example, else what way is there left to stop detracting mouths, and to vindicate the name of Christ from the reproaches of the world? How can wisdom be justified of her children, except it be this way? By what means shall we cut off occasion from such as desire occasion, but by regulating our lives by Christ's example. The world hath eyes to see what we practice, as well as ears to hear what we profess. Therefore either show the consistency between your profession and practice, or you can never hope to vindicate the name and honor of the Lord Jesus" (John Flavel, Puritan).

From all that has now been before us we may draw the following inferences. First, if all who claim a saving interest in Christ are strictly bound to imitate Him, then it follows that Christianity is very unjustly charged by the world with the evils and scandals of empty professors. Nothing can be more unreasonable, for Christianity severely censures loose and scandalous actions in all professors, and therefore is not to be blamed for them. "For the grace of God that bringeth salvation hath appeared to all men, teaching us that denying ungodliness and worldly lusts, we should live soberly, righteously, and godly in this present world" (Titus 2:11-12). Really, it is an argument greatly in favor of Christianity that even wicked men covet the name of it, though they only cloak their sins under it.

Second, if all professors forfeit their claim to a saving interest in Christ who endeavor not, sincerely and earnestly, to imitate Him in the holiness of His life, then how small a number of real Christians are there in the world! If flowery talking without strict walking, if common profession without holy practice, if Church membership without denying self and treading the narrow way, were sufficient to constitute a Christian, then a considerable percentage of earth's population would be entitled to that name. But if Christ owns none but those who follow the example that He left, then His flock is indeed a little one. The vast majority of those who claim to be Christians have a name to live, but are dead (Rom. 6:13). The demands of Christ are too rigid for them. They prefer the broad road where the majority are found.

Third, what blessed times we should witness if true Christianity once generally obtained and prevailed in the world! How it would humble the proud, mellow the self-willed, and spiritualize those who are carnal. A perverse world has often charged Christianity with being the cause of all the tumult in it; whereas nothing but pure Christianity, in the power of it, can cure those epidemics of evil. If the great majority of our fellows were regenerated by the Spirit and brought to walk after Christ in holiness, living in meekness and self-denial, then our prisons would be closed, armies and navies done away with, jealousies and animosities be removed, and the wilderness and solitary places be glad. The desert would rejoice and blossom as the rose. That is what constitutes the great difference between heaven and a world that lieth in the wicked one. Holiness is the very atmosphere of the former, whereas it is hated and banned here.

Fourth, it also follows that real Christians are the best companions. It is a blessed thing to fellowship with those who genuinely seek to follow the example of Christ. The holiness, heavenly mindedness, and spiritual graces which were in Him are, in their measure, to be found in all of His true disciples. They show the praises of Him who called them out of darkness into light. Something of the fruit of the Spirit is to be seen in all those whom He indwells. Yet it must be remembered there is a great deal of difference between one Christian and another, that the best is sanctified only in part. If there is something engaging and sweet, there is also that which is distasteful and bitter in the most mature saints. This is what gives us occasion to forbear one another in love. Nevertheless, notwithstanding all infirmities and corruptions, the Lord's people are the best companions on this earth. Happy are they who now enjoy fellowship with those in whom can be discerned the likeness of Christ.

Fifth, if no man's claim to being Christ's is warranted except so far as he is walking according to Him, then how groundless and worthless are the expectations of all unsanctified persons, who walk after their own lusts.

None are more forward to claim the privileges of religion than those that reject the duties of it; multitudes hope to be saved by Christ, who yet refuse to be governed by Him. But such hopes have no Scripture warrant to support them; yea, they have many Scripture testimonies against them. "Know ye not that the unrighteous shall not inherit the kingdom of God? Be not deceived; neither fornicators, nor idolaters, nor adulterers, nor effeminate, nor abusers of themselves with mankind, nor thieves, nor covetous, nor drunkards, nor revilers, nor extortioners, shall inherit the kingdom of God" (1 Cor. 6:9). O how many thousand vain hopes are laid in the dust, and how many thousand souls are sentenced to Hell by this one Scripture! (John Flavel, 1660).

Then how it behooves those of us who profess to be Christians to "be not conformed to this world," but to be "transformed by the renewing of our minds" (Rom. 12:2). How we should strive to follow Christ's steps. That should be the great business of our lives, as it is the chief scope of the Gospel. If Christ has conformed Himself to us by taking upon Him our nature, how reasonable it is that we should conform ourselves to Him in a way of obedience. He came under the Law for our sakes (Gal. 4:4), the least we can do in return is to gladly take His yoke upon us. It was Christ's abasement to conform Himself to those who were infinitely beneath Him; it will be our advancement to conform ourselves to Him who is so high above us. Surely the love of Christ must constrain us to spare no efforts to "grow up into him in all things" (Eph. 4:15).

If we will be conformed to Him in glory, how logical it is that we should now conform ourselves to Him in holiness. "We shall be like him, for we shall see him as he is" (1 John 3:2), like Him not only in our souls, but also our bodies too will be transformed like unto His (Phil. 3:21). What a motive this is to bring us into conformity with Christ here, especially since our conformity to Him in holiness is the evidence of our conformity to Him in glory (Rom. 6:5). The conformity of our lives to Christ is our highest excellence in this world, for the measure of our grace is to be estimated by this rule. So far as we imitate Christ, and no farther, are we of any real help to those around us; contrariwise, the less we be conformed to Christ, the greater hindrances and stumbling blocks we are both to the saved and unsaved. What a solemn consideration this is! How it should drive us to our knees, seeking grace to be closer followers of Christ.

"That ye should walk worthy of God, who hath called you into his kingdom and glory" (1 Thess. 2:12). By "worthiness" the apostle had no reference to what is meritorious, but to that decorum which befits a Christian. As Davenant pointed out, "The word 'worthy' as used in Scripture does not always denote an exact proportion of equality between one thing and another, but a certain suitableness and fitness which excludes inconsistency." To walk worthy of God is to walk as Christ walked, and any deviation from that standard is a reflection on our profession and a reproach upon Him. It is for our own peace that we be conformed to Christ's pattern. The answer of a good conscience and the smile of God's approbation are rich compensation for denying the flesh. A comfortable death is the ordinary close of a holy life. "Mark the perfect man, and behold the upright: for the end of that man is peace" (Ps. 37:37).

In drawing to a conclusion let us consider a few lines of comfort to those who are cast down by the realization of how far short they come of measuring up to the standard Christ set before them. According to the yearnings of the new nature, you have sincerely endeavored to follow Christ's example. But being weak in grace and meeting with much opposition from the flesh and temptations from the devil, you have been frequently turned aside from the holy purposes of your honest hearts, to the great discouragement of your souls. You can say with David, "O that my ways were directed to keep thy statutes!" (Ps. 119:5): you have tried hard to follow after holiness, "If by any means" you might attain it. But your efforts have been repeatedly thwarted, your aspirations dashed, and you have to cry,

"O wretched man that I am! who shall deliver me?" (Rom. 7:24).

First, let us assure the genuinely exercised soul that such defects in obedience do not invalidate your justification, or affect your acceptance with and standing before God. Your justification is built not upon your obedience, but upon Christ's. However imperfect you are, you are "complete in him" (Col. 2:10). Woe to Abraham, Moses, David, or Paul if their justification depended upon their own holiness and good works. Let not your sad failures dampen your joy in Christ, but rather be increasingly thankful for His robe of righteousness. Second, your heart anguish over your unlikeness to Christ, instead of being a proof that you are less sanctified than those who do not grieve over their lack of conformity to Him, evidences that you are more sanctified than they; for it shows you are better acquainted with your heart than they are, have a deep loathing of sin, and love God more. The most distinguished saints have made the bitterest lamentation on this account (Ps. 38:4).

Third, the Holy Spirit makes an excellent use of your infirmities and turns your failures into spiritual advantages. By those very defects He hides pride from your eyes, subdues your self-righteousness, causes you to appreciate more deeply the riches of free grace and place a higher value on the blood of the Lamb. By your many falls He makes you to long more ardently for heaven, and gradually reconciles you to the prospect of death. The more a holy soul is buffeted by sin and Satan, the more sincerely he will cry, "O that I had wings like a dove! for then would I fly away, and be at rest" (Ps. 55:6). "O the blessed chemistry of Heaven, to extract such mercies out of such miseries" (John Flavel), to make sweet flowers spring up out of such bitter roots. Fourth, your infirmities do not break the bond of the everlasting covenant, that holds firm, notwithstanding your many defects and corruptions. "Iniquities prevail against me" said David, yet in the same breath he added, "thou shalt purge them away" (Ps. 65:3).

Fifth, though the defects of your obedience are grievous to God, yet your deep sorrows for them are well pleasing in His sight. "The sacrifices of God are a broken spirit: a broken and a contrite heart, O God, thou wilt not despise" (Ps. 51:17). Sixth, your grief is a conformity to Christ, for He was "the Man of sorrows." If He suffered because of our sins, shall we not be made to weep over them. Seventh, "Though God have left many defects to humble you, yet He hath given many things to comfort. This is a comfort, that the desire of thy soul is to God and the remembrance of His name. This is a comfort, that thy sins are not thy delight as once they were, but thy shame and sorrow. This is a comfort, that thy case is not singular, but more or less the same complaints and sorrows are found in all gracious souls through the world" (John Flavel, to whom we are indebted for much of the above).

Made in the USA
Coppell, TX
18 April 2022

76734959R00075